HOLD THE LINE

THE ESSENTIAL GUIDE TO PROTECTING YOUR LAW ENFORCEMENT RELATIONSHIP

CYNDI DOYLE, LPC-S

Printed in the United States of America

First Printing, 2021

ISBN e-book 9780578828848

ISBN Print 9780578828824

Code4Couples®

www.Code4Couples.com

www.HoldtheLineBook.com

WHAT PEOPLE ARE SAYING ABOUT "HOLD THE LINE"

Cyndi Doyle's "Hold the Line," is a remarkable, intriguing book, written with insightful observation, unflinching honesty, and her wonderful sense of humor. More importantly, it provides the tools necessary to help officers to emotionally survive and build resilience in their personal relationships with others. This book provides a tremendous service to law enforcement in fomenting a healthy, positive mindset. I highly recommend this book for the law enforcement community.

Jack C. Perritt

Dallas Police Department, Retired

Executive Director, Strike International-CMC

If you are a law enforcement spouse or officer and haven't read this book, you are missing out! This book spoke to my soul as a police spouse and I had so many "ah-ha" moments reading it. Not only was it relatable but Cyndi gave reasons as to WHY I was feeling the way I was. Highly recommend!

Rebecca Lynn

Founder of Proud Police Wife and Author www.ProudPoliceWife.com

As someone who has never worked as a law enforcement officer or a first responder. As someone who is not married to one one, I had trusted my training and experience as a rehabilitation counsellor to help me inform my work with people who don't just 'do' this work but 'live' this work.

And while I'm good at what I do, can develop empathy well and genuinely want to know how to best serve all my clients, reading Hold The Line has opened my eyes to what I don't know.

The lifestyle, culture, social expectations and personal responses of being a first responder can't be book learned. We need resources that add to the existing body of knowledge in very real and tangible ways.

Cyndi's use of storytelling, personal experience and theoretical frameworks is an excellent example of evidence based practice informing her work and then sharing it with us.

The relationships I have with LEO friends has improved, and my work with people who are no longer LEO's has improved because of this book.

I highly recommend any health professional of any discipline read this and access the resources Cyndi has on offer.

Jo Muirhead, Consultant Rehabilitation Counsellor

BHlthSc (Rehabilitation Counseling) MASRC CDAA

www.JoMuirhead.com

Cyndi Doyle's "Hold The Line" is a must read for first responder couples. This book incorporates honest, real world experiences of a law enforcement couple which are reinforced with psychological analysis and practical advice. This book should be utilized throughout the career and marriage of first responder couples. By reading this book a couple will learn not only to hold the line but how to walk that line together.

Cathy & Javi - That Peer Support Couple

www.cathyandjavi.com

Damn. I feel like Cyndi has been following me taking copious notes about the way law enforcement can impact your life...*on* and *off* the job. After reading Gilmartin's *Emotional Survival for Law Enforcement,* the Wife and I set upon a new course to improve our relationship. Now that I'm on the other side of retirement from law enforcement, I can say with confidence Gilmartin's book should be on your bookshelf...right next to this one. Cyndi offers insight Gilmartin can't: the Insider View. With that insider insight, Cyndi offers wisdom and guidance in a way only someone who has walked in your shoes can. Cyndi is authentic, transparent, and offers you empathy without judgement, ulterior motive, or making you feel like you're somehow broken and unfixable.

You will see where Cyndi and her law enforcement husband have failed and succeeded. You will be able to learn from their experiences without necessarily having to experience them yourself. You will have access to a number of strategies designed specifically with your law enforcement marriage in mind. Sound guidance offered from someone who has seen it, lived it, and lived to talk about it.

It's never too late to take the first step to improve your relationship or avoid some rather large pitfalls before you fall ass over teakettle into them.

Cheers to Cyndi for being strong and confident enough to write the book.

Cheers to you for having the wherewithal to pick it up and read it.

Jason "MotorCop" Hoschouer

SF Bay Area Police Officer, Retired

Podcast Host at WYERadio.com

When Cyndi asked me to read and review her book, I was honored and intrigued. I have been working with couples as a professional therapist for 28 years and specialize in working with first responders. Cyndi has given professionals and law enforcement couples a priceless gift. Cyndi combines her personal experience of being a LEO spouse, her many years of marriage and her professional expertise of working with couples and individuals to bring together this book which is a legacy manuscript. Any professional therapist will be educated by her sharing of her own experiences. Cyndi writes in a way of wit, knowledge and just down-to-earth solutions which will help couples to see themselves and apply these practical tools in their lives.

It is an honor to recommend "Hold The Line" to my LEO couples.

Kate Pieper, Licensed Marriage Family Therapist

EMDRIA Certified EMDR Therapist & EMDRIA Approved Consultant in Training

Certified Critical Incident Stress Management

Hold The Line, is a must read book for everyone who loves, supports, knows or is a first responder family.

This book is a game changer! Cyndi Doyle vulnerably shares wisdom gained the long, hard way- so you don't have to!

As a first responder spouse and first responder couples counsellor, Cyndi gets it! I laughed out loud so many times reading this book as I felt like I was reading my very own first responder marriage love story and the stories of so many first responder families I am honored to work with.

My hope is this book finds its way into every recruit class, first responder home and counseling office. This book will absolutely impact first responder families and those who support them by normalizing, empowering and increasing awareness, connection, compassion and hope.

ACKNOWLEDGMENTS

To my parents, Jim & Shirley Brinkman for your love and support, James Brinkman, inspiring your big sister to leap, and Brandy Stiles, my ultimate cheerleader.

To my friends and colleagues who have inspired, supported, pushed, believed, inspired, and coached me along the way.

A special acknowledgement to Jo Muirhead who said it needed to be written, Dr. Amy Fortney Parks for her brain consultation, and Adam Davis for editing the hot mess of a manuscript.

CONTENTS

INTRODUCTION

I was crying. I was crying and I was pissed. I was tired of always accommodating, being understanding, and feeling second. I wanted to know when it was going to be my turn. When exactly was the focus going to shift away from the department? He'd been in for twelve years! Hadn't he made it to a point where he could back off a little? Hadn't he paid his dues? Didn't he realize that it wasn't all about work? Didn't work realize that he had a life?

I was in full-on temper tantrum mode. They were rare, as I am usually super easy going and accommodating. I was *done* accommodating. I was *done* sucking it up and putting my needs aside. I was *done* being kind. I was *done*. I hit a wall and I hit it hard; and he didn't even know. We had been here before and it resulted in both of us being passive-aggressive, fighting for control over time, and over influence of each other. It had resulted in some not so nice interactions but almost always me accommodating and being hurt.

One situation that stands out even now was a Thanksgiving about a year before I hit the wall. He *finally* had off on the holiday and I was determined to have him go with me to my parent's house four hours away. I was done asking him to accompany me and flat out said,

"We are going to Austin this year for Thanksgiving." I remember he gave me an excuse about work but I don't exactly recall what it was. I knew that I had challenged him by doing so. I had tried to take control. I didn't realize just how much doing that would impact us. I went to Thanksgiving in Austin alone only to receive an email from my lovely (and I mean that!) mother-in-law the next day saying that they had a very lovely Thanksgiving at my house and how much they missed me at the dinner. It was a betrayal. I remember holding on to that until I got back home, saw him, and confronted him with the email. It made me question a lot.

Trust was so important in our relationship as we saw each other little with his shifts and my hours in private practice. Were there other ways he had lied or stretched the truth. Was he *really* needed at the department? What else was I being naive about? It wounded me. If I remember correctly, there was little conversation for several days.

I was now hitting the wall because he had told me "no" to going on my parent's 50th anniversary cruise. The department was requiring him to get his degree. He couldn't miss classes in October when the cruise was scheduled. Plus, he had responsibilities to the department and they were short-staffed, again. He was apologetic, but my thought was "how convenient!" Yes, it all sounds very logical. I could tell my brain, "It makes sense. Of course, he has to go to school and cover shifts." My emotional brain said, "F*** all this f***ing *shit* and the f***ing department! It's not f***ing fair! I do the right thing! I'm supportive and understanding! This is not fair and I'm ***done***!"

But he had no idea.

While he was getting those 10,000 little cuts at work, I was experiencing them at home. I did a great job masking my wounds by being super supportive. Sure, go to the training, go to school, pick up that extra shift, be on-call, stay late for reports, do that extra thing for the chief. Inside I was shutting down. The bricks were being laid and the wall was getting higher and higher. I dove into my work and built a badass practice. I was no longer investing in my relationship. I didn't want to be disappointed. I didn't want to be hurt. So, I walled up. Sure, we were having sex. I mean, a girl has needs too. Yes, I was still being kind and caring. I'm a pretty nice and thoughtful person according to just about anyone you will ask. I didn't leave my relationship but I was no longer *in* my relationship; not in the way that I was counseling my couples to be. I started to see that. It didn't make me proud, but I wasn't sure how to turn the tide.

I didn't leave my relationship, but I was no longer in my relationship

I was resentful. I was resentful toward him. I was resentful of the department. I was resentful toward myself for being *so* accommodating and not being more vocal. I thought maybe I should have been more angry. That seemed to work for other wives for a time, only to be called "crazy" or a "bitch" behind their backs and sometimes end in divorce. They blamed the career. "He was a different person when I met him. Now, he can be such an asshole." No one explained to us what was going on. No one mentored us.

WHAT DIDN'T WORK

We were in this together from the beginning. He went through the academy while we were dating. We got married and a week after we got back from our honeymoon, he was picked up by a department. I was so proud of him. I was proud to say my husband was a police officer. In my mind, I had hit the jackpot (I am now back to thinking this way daily!); this man cooked *and* cleaned the dishes, was smart, made me feel safe and like a queen, told me how beautiful I was, thought I was sexy as hell, *and* put the toilet seat down! Now, he had a stable, steady job that he could retire from. Cool! We are set!

At first, he was super excited about his job and would share everything with me. All the calls, what stupid things citizens had done, the details of an arrest, a warrant that was being served. I was *in* the loop. At times I was thinking, "Dude, alright with all the work conversation," but I didn't dissuade it. Then slowly that faded. Conversation became more minimal. We wouldn't see each other because of shifts. In fact, there was probably a good almost five years where we saw each other about six hours a week, and not consecutively. I took things in stride. I accommodated. I changed my schedule to make sure I was home when he was home (this is still a difficult mindset for me to break.) I was understanding of him needing to work overtime, especially that 18 months when the department lost a ton of officers and he was one of only two or three field training officers (FTOs) having to train every new person in the department.

I admired him (I still do; deeply) and because of that I was accommodating of his moods and bursts of irritation that were not there when we dated. I told myself it was stress and he deals with a lot and let it go. He would come home and sleep and at other times do nothing. He didn't really want to leave the house when he was off. He didn't want to run into people that he had arrested or encountered on a call. I would push to go out on a date but then give in because I thought I was being a "good wife." In actuality, I would find out later that I was enabling his behavior. I was also feeling disappointed and sad, and not talking about it because I didn't want to appear unsupportive. I would bring things up every now and then only to have my feelings swept away due to the impact or importance of the job.

Anger outbursts and eggshells increased in our house. I was uncomfortable with irritation and anger so I would try to make sure things were perfect. I would get quiet when he would have an outburst and sometimes cry in the bathroom. In my head, it was me or us that was causing these. I never imagined it was the impact or effect of being in law enforcement.

MY LIGHTBULB MOMENT

After hitting that wall, there was a moment of clarity in the middle of a silent internal melt down. Something clicked in my head. As a licensed counselor, I was taught "you have to meet your client where they are at." In a nutshell, this means you have to work to see the place where your client is and understand their world in such a way that they feel completely heard and understood.

We suspend judgment in an effort to know how the "story" of their life has shaped their views, their responses, their defense mechanisms, and their coping and sometimes survival skills. I realized I was *not* extending this same courtesy and skill to the one person I had committed to love. I was being judgy, critical, and personalizing when I needed to be getting into his head, understanding, and empathizing. I realized I had a skill that I paid *good* money for (my Master's Degree) that I was not using to my benefit.

I realized I was not extending this same courtesy and skill to the one person I had committed to love.

One clue fell into my lap at a counseling conference and I texted my husband, "Hey do you OODA?" His response was something like, "Where the hell are you?" I was excited to come home and share what I learned. He was probably underwhelmed. That moment, that piece of information, helped me to know that there must be things that neither he nor I was aware of. I started asking more questions about his training and books his mentors were recommending. I started looking at the books and looking at their references. I read *Emotional Survival for Law Enforcement* and light bulbs went on everywhere. I started thinking back to our relationship and seeing how the career was impacting my husband, our relationship, and *me*.

It was great to have all the information but over time as it started to marinate in my brain, I realized it wasn't enough just to understand what was going on in his brain. It opened up conversation between the two of us. He had seen officers get divorced, have affairs, make poor decisions, and spend *way* more money than they earned only to work overtime to make up for it and it impacted their relationship. He had tried to warn some of the rookies coming in to BOLO ("be on the lookout".) We recognized our own struggles and saw them in others.

The more conversation we had, much of that on the porch having wine or out in the field in a hunting blind, the more I was able to see through my husband's eyes and understand his brain. The more things marinated in my brain, the more I was able to understand the underpinning of what was really going on and how it was redirecting us in a direction we did not want to go. I realized that I did not want to just succumb to the impact of the career. He may have thought my psycho-mumbo-jumbo was ridiculous, but he was listening and through the last several years he has been willing to take a second look at the psychology underneath the career and the impact. He was also willing to understand what it was like to be a spouse of a law enforcement officer.

I realized that I did not want to just succumb to the impact of the career.

In a way, this is our love story. It's the story of how we didn't know what we didn't know. It's the story of how we grew distant, experienced pain, and found our way back to each other in a deeper more meaningful way, but not without both of us owning our part of how we allowed this career in law enforcement to disrupt us separately and as a couple. It's the legacy we hope to leave behind. A legacy of research-based information and personal stories to normalize experiences, educate, and empower you to create the relationship you want and need while working in law enforcement.

WHAT WE ALL KNOW.... BUT WHY?

We were newlyweds when my husband started his career. Honestly, my only concern at that time was "don't die." I made a stand and told him I was comfortable with him working anywhere in the Dallas-Fort Worth area as long as it wasn't Dallas or Fort Worth. My mindset was if he wasn't in the big city, nothing bad could happen to him. Yes, I was naive and you can insert your chuckle or eye roll here. I know now that many times smaller departments are stretched thin and lack resources they need in equipment and personnel to stay and remain safe.

Geographic areas can be vast with few people being able to come and provide back-up in a timely manner. Financial resources in the form of a tax base can be small; therefore, support in the way of insurance providing assistance for physical and mental well-being is limited or non-existent. But, in my mind, being at a smaller suburban department sounded safer. We both admit to being naive to a lot of aspects of how this career would impact both of us individually and our relationship. It's something we look back on with a feeling of, "bless their hearts."

We didn't see a threat to our marriage. People told him about the super high divorce rate of 75%. We were shocked but could not imagine what was happening that would cause couples to split. We figured maybe it was cheating and moved past it. I mean, as long as we loved each other, we thought it would be fine. Right? We simply didn't know what we didn't know.

We simply didn't know what we didn't know.

THE DIVORCE RATE IS BULLSHIT.

You will see numbers tossed around regarding the divorce rate. The highest I've come across is 75%. That then gets validated when you hear officers and couples getting divorced, affairs within the department, and hear about officers that have been married three, four, or five times. It's scary and the fear of divorce gets fed when we start to see relationships fall apart or see the posts on social media. The fact is that the divorce rate is a myth and is old information that was passed down, generation to generation, to other rookies and officers. There are some departments that have a culture that promotes affairs simply by assuming it is part of the career. There are others that do not tolerate such behavior. The divorce rate that continues to be perpetuated is based upon old research from the 1960s and 1970s. A more recent [1]study from 2010 examined law enforcement divorce rates compared to many different careers. The findings showed that the divorce rate in the general category of law enforcement was actually lower than the national rate of divorce which, by the way, is also dropping. It was noted that compared to the 1960s and 1970s, couples often live together before deciding to get married and the average age of people getting married is higher than in the past. So, not only is the overall divorce rate dropping but those in law enforcement are *below* the national average. While that is terrific information, there is much that impacts our relationships and without understanding and ownership by both, we are doomed to be one of the statistics.

There are other myths I have heard over the years regarding police marriages, and they include things about abuse, alcoholism, addiction, affairs, mental health issues, and other forms of various nefarious and bad behavior. Do these exist in law enforcement relationships? Absolutely. What I have learned is to really check things out before I go jumping to conclusions.

It's easy to say that there are a certain percentage of law enforcement relationships/marriages that have something happen. How does that differ from other relationships or professions, is it based on research, and how *old* is the research? There will always be unhealthy relationships. A career in law enforcement can impact some of that. I learned to be more discerning when it came to reading information that is available on the internet or social media. If we look for something, we will find it. Be careful what you look for!

SHIFT WORK.

In any industry, shift work impacts the individual and relationships. The norm in most societies is to work during the day and come home at night. I remember reading a blog post from someone one day on suggested bonding activities for your relationship. It included things like having meals every night at the dinner table, exercising together, and having a nightly ritual that included going to bed together. I laughed, very loud. People stared.

The first problem with shift work is that your norms are not the norms for many other couples. Days off are different. When the rest of your friends are having a weekend with their spouse; you may be alone. I have often had to go to social gatherings alone because of shifts. Oh! And let's not forget the holidays! There is nothing more annoying than hearing people think they are original or clever with some form of the "I'm beginning to wonder if you have a husband" comment. Or your family telling you for the umpteenth time that your spouse, "Just needs to request leave time and stand up for themselves" or "Just tell the department he can't work then." Ha!

I've heard several forms of these. After years of hearing it, I would laugh it off, be annoyed, get defensive, irritated, and think how insensitive the comment really was. It honestly hurt and made me feel different and more alone than I already felt. I didn't *enjoy* going to your party/event/holiday alone, but I thought it was better than being rude and not showing up at all. My husband was sometimes honestly excited that he got out of some social obligations and other times longed to attend a dinner party with friends. We both had our own realities of the situation. Some of my/our closer friends really understood. Others we drifted away from. I don't think it was until recently that my family really understood what it was like for me. I play it tough a lot of times. One day I had enough and it all came spilling out.

Weekends are a "thing." People have [2]rituals and traditions for the weekend. But when your weekend is in the middle of the week, no one is available to get together to hang out. You wind up spending it alone, maybe even without your spouse because they are at work. Some people make the most of it, and some people get bored and turn to less helpful coping skills. Weekends are a ritual that is established early on in our life as a time to relax. They are times to connect with your family or friends. It provides a challenge when you do not have that ritual of connection to fall back on weekly. My husband and I did not have a weekend together for several years. We have agreed upon it being probably about five years. He worked 6 PM to 2 AM and I worked 8-5. He would be asleep when I left and I would be asleep when he got home. He would have off on a weekday and make dinner. We'd have a couple of hours together to talk, catch up, or have sex. It wasn't much but we savored what we could. I always felt like he was half there. I didn't know why until years later.

SLEEP.

In addition to the schedule, shift work often comes with a change in sleeping patterns. I knew sleep was going to be an issue with shift work, but I didn't think how it would impact my or our life. In the years that we were on different schedules, we saw little of each other. I would busy myself with various activities and many times being purposefully out of the house and not coming back too soon for fear of the dogs starting to bark. I would strategically plan my outings, trying to do things in the house for a while and then venturing out around late morning knowing that I wouldn't be done with errands until he would potentially be waking up.

One of the hobbies I took up for a while was scrapbooking. I was in the middle of designing some pages and reading about how to document daily life to create memorable and interesting scrapbooks. I remember laughing a little and then grabbing my camera. I slowly and quietly opened the master bedroom door and crept in, kneeled at the side of the bed, and took pictures of my husband sleeping. I blew it up to an 8x10 when I had it processed. I'm sure someone got a kick out of it! My idea was that it was going to be two pages in the scrapbook because him sleeping was such a *large* part of our lives.

Sleep is vital. It is your body's way of hitting a reset button. When you sleep your brain activates the glymphatic system, which is basically the brain's sewer system. The chemicals released go into all the little crevices of the brain to clean out the negative aspects of your day and help you process things that happened during the day. Sleep lowers cortisol, our stress hormones, and at least attempts to return our body to a somewhat healthier state. It is a vital part of not just our physical health, but our mental health to have sleep.

Our bodies are also set up to have a natural rhythm, the circadian rhythm, that helps us to wake and sleep. All of our rhythms are different but none of them are set up to work in the middle of the night.

The truth is that the sleeping environment that our law enforcement officers need to get great sleep is hard to recreate during the day.

We outfit bedrooms with blackout curtains and sound machines. We as spouses tiptoe around, try to hold off on noisy housework chores, keep kids on the other side of the house or outside when they are home, put signs outside on our doors and tell people not to ring the doorbell, and go bananas when the delivery driver shows up and knocks anyway. The truth is that the sleeping environment that our law enforcement officers need to get great sleep is hard to recreate during the day. Officers try to stay on schedule with their sleep but also make the decision to adjust when they are off to have some time with spouses, family, kids, and friends. Lack of sleep or lack of *good* sleep prevents our bodies from being healed from events and impacts our mood.

The truth is that the sleeping environment that creates great sleep for is hard to recreate for officers that need to sleep during the day. I don't mean the physical wounds, I mean the mental wounds. The ones we can't see, at least not initially. The longer they go without being able to heal from these wounds and the more exposure they have, the greater the impact on their personality, mood, and their vulnerability to being susceptible to greater mental-emotional wounds. Officers and spouses want to feel connected to each other. Having shared experiences creates oxytocin which bonds us as a couple. Without those shared experiences, relationships can feel stale and vulnerabilities for outside influences can occur. What I and other couples fail to realize is the slow slide and impact that shift work is having. We don't have a choice so we just keep functioning and operating, feeling lonely, disconnected, slightly resentful, and maybe even a little sorry for ourselves and/or our spouse. We are aware and we make the best of it trying to create connection when we can, but also feeling disappointed at the same time.

WORRY, ANXIETY, AND FEAR.... OH MY!

The two primary feelings I hear from police spouses are fear and loneliness. I know for certain I did not grow up thinking, "Gosh, I can't wait to find the partner of my dreams, get married (or not), sleep in my bed alone, be alone much of the time, and worry about whether they are going to make it home after their shift!" Yup, said no little girl or boy *ever*! It's human to be worried and hate being alone. This doesn't just go for the spouse side though. Officers also don't love the fact that they are away and cannot protect or be there with their family, especially at times of uncertainty or disruption. I'm currently writing this in the middle of COVID-19 and my husband would like it if I wore a bubble suit and/or PPE every time I left the house. I often work evenings seeing clients at the office and he is not too fond of me walking out of the office in a pitch-black parking lot. Then again, neither am I. He worries about me as much as I worry about him. He wasn't crazy about having days off and not getting to spend it with me as much as I felt the same about being alone when he was on shift. The feelings are human.

Sometimes those feelings take over in not such a good way. Our brain (you'll hear a lot of that phrase in this book) likes to create chaos and make up disaster scenarios. Case in point: How many times have you texted someone, not received a response in what your brain deems as timely, and then sat and wondered if you pissed them off in some way? Yup, me too. Our brain is wired for survival! There is an *entire* section of your brain, the limbic system, dedicated to helping predict danger. It's where your fight or flight system originates. It's actually now, fight, flight, freeze, and fawn. I'll explain more about that later. For now, let's just say those negative feelings can cause us to behave in ways that are not congruent or true with our character or loving behavior, coming out many times as anxiety, depression, anger, and/or control.

So, great! We can't be with our spouses. One walks into danger on a daily basis. The other could potentially be in danger and you can't protect them. It makes for some really great material for your brain to be creative. Your brain also likes to use your previous experiences to create stories of what is going on in the current situation.

One of the most popular conflicts with law enforcement couples is communication and/or lack of communication when an officer is on shift. I've had several versions of this situation in my office or emails from people.

Here's how it goes: Officer is on duty and texts the spouse to find out what's going on in their world. No response... no response... Officer texts again with no response after several minutes. Officer texts again with growing concern and the text gets a little more stern. No response again after several minutes. The officer then texts, this time with anger due to the non-response and may even say something snarky. Spouse gets to their phone and sees several text messages first starting out with checking in and then with more annoyance and irritation. The spouse, who was out walking the dog and left the phone in the house, is now irritated at the exchange and feels controlled.

Or, another version of this is...

Spouse texts officers on duty to find out when they are going to be home. Officer texts back that they have an abundance of paperwork that needs to get done and are going to be late. The spouse thinks, "how long does paperwork take" and texts thirty minutes later.

Again, the officer responds saying they are doing paperwork and will be home later. The spouse reads this and starts thinking, "I bet he is talking to that new dispatcher!" and a little while later sends another text or maybe even a stream of upset texts.

I'm not innocent of this! I have certainly called dispatch on occasion to make sure my husband was still there and ok when I didn't hear from him an hour after his shift ended. Things happen. We ***know*** this, but our brain likes to create situations and stories around situations in the effort to prepare us for bad things. Not always helpful!

We are so used to immediate responses, our brain starts to create stories around situations when we don't get a response. We create reasons they are not responding, and many times those reasons are not the reality.

OVERIDENTIFICATION

It was exciting for both my husband and myself when he started in his department. I was excited for him to be doing something he believed in; he would come home and tell me the stories of what happened in his field training, each experience a new and exciting one. So many stories with so much detail, some of which I didn't get and would get lost in, but I would try my best to understand what was exciting and SOPs which determined how he handles certain situations. There was a point, although it was more of a slow slide, in which I realized that being a police officer was no longer what he did for a living and more about who he was. It impacted the way he thought and what he did.

Behavior and beliefs were bleeding over into home. I knew he was changing. His friends were changing and the way he viewed friends and family and society was changing in a negative way. He was happy primarily when he was talking about work to someone from work. Many other topics were met with small sentences with not much elaboration, but bring up something tactical and he was all over it. Now, I will say that my husband has always been into guns as he was a hunter. Early in our relationship, I was going to bed and I saw him holding up a Guns and Ammo magazine sideways, the way you would hold up a centerfold. I remember leering at him and asking him what he was reading. He looked up and replied, "ballistics charts." I continued to leer at him and said something like, "Oh really! You must think I'm an idiot! What are you really looking at!?" He spun the magazine around and said, "ballistics charts!" So, yeah, he was already into those things but it ramped up to a new level.

We are so used to immediate responses, our brain starts to create stories around situations when we don't get a response.

I didn't really see anything wrong with enjoying work so much and talking about it. I did notice that when we tried to go out with people that were not in the field, conversation would fall flat. Part of that I didn't find so weird as I struggle to make "small talk" with people at times. However, I did start to notice that it was impacting our relationships with others and activities. He would watch over situations as opposed to being able to enjoy himself.

I could tell at times that he would think some people's view of the world was ridiculous. People would also ask him stupid questions like, "so what's the worst call you've been on?" They didn't get it. It was annoying as hell but I tried to understand what he was saying. I didn't really think much of the fact that all of his friends were other police officers and couples we spent time with were other police couples because they "got it." I saw how others went overboard in their identity and justified our situation by comparing to others. It was about pride and being #bluefamily. I didn't see the "big deal."

I didn't even know to be aware of or worry about overidentification. In short, overidentification is when you lose your sense of self and objectivity due to identifying with someone or something in an excessive way. This is different than simply identifying as something that you do or picking up aspects or traits of the job. I identify as a counselor and my skills and training come with me, much to the despair of my husband at times. It happens.

Overidentification can be a slow slide, happening slowly bit by bit, abandoning or turning against friends not in law enforcement, changing interests to only law enforcement related type activities, leaving the house always armed, having black cars detailed with blue pinstripes, and wearing clothing that would be considered law enforcement clothing, you know the tactical pants and polo shirt combo. (I think it's funny that we can go anywhere on vacation and my husband is surprised when people ask if he's a cop. Now, I just remind him that he's wearing the off duty uniform.) Some officers overidentify with being a police officer to overcome an inadequacy they have in themselves, to feel more powerful, in control, or prove something to themselves or others.

Overidentification is when you lose your sense of self and objectivity due to identifying with someone or something in an excessive way.

I worry that families and spouses struggling with overidentification will grow as the pride for our officers and divide/hate for officers grows in some places in our country and the world. Would you believe I have not one police-related home decor item hanging in my house? My thought on that? It takes up so much space in our lives, it doesn't need to invade our home even more. I AM the wife of a law enforcement officer. I have a few t-shirts supporting the "blue." My husband also has a shirt that he wears proudly that says, "Real men marry counselors" and yes, I bought it for him.

We identify by many other things rather than solely a police couple. There is a balance between pride and overidentifying. Having decor and other police couples in your life is not only acceptable, but I would encourage it. Yet you also need other friends and other ways to identify. I have known spouses whose officer had to leave or chose to leave the field. The spouses were then left with a sudden loss of self due to their identification of being a law enforcement wife. They adopted their spouse's career as their identity, had all the home decor, joined the auxiliary, and only had law enforcement friends and spouses. They were lost and pissed at their spouses for doing what was right for them.

CRITICAL INCIDENTS, TRAUMA, & SUICIDE

Probably the greatest fear that spouses have is their spouse or significant other being involved in a critical incident of some kind. We know that there is a daily possibility. Many of us get really good at putting it to the side in some way. We come up with sayings like, "trust the training" and "his purpose is to come home every night." There is no preparing for an incident or the call that says, "He's ok but.... " or "Don't panic but...." Some departments ask officers how they want to handle notifications to their spouses and others have no protocol. I strongly suggest you talk about this as a couple. I am grateful to have only been through minor incidents with my husband and to have worked with officers and spouses that needed help recovering from more critical incidents. I can tell the call, no matter what the incident, results in the same physiological response such as shock, and fight or flight. The first situation involved my husband being hit by another vehicle. Dispatch called me and said, "Mrs. Doyle, everything is ok but your husband's been in a collision and he's on the way to the ER." I remember sitting and staring at the other person in my office (I worked at a non-profit at this time) and not knowing what to do. After what seemed like about 30 minutes, I called his mom and had her meet me at the hospital.

The second time, one of his chief's called. "Hey Cyndi, it's Mark. I don't want you to panic but..." I looked at my clients and calmly told them I had to go and drove to the hospital near his department. The difference in my reaction was two-fold. First, I was way more seasoned the second time around. I clicked into "fix it" mode and there was no time to feel. Second, the fact that someone I knew called and called me by my first name meant the world to me. It made a difference. It's worth starting a conversation at your agency if there isn't one already.

Not every incident is trauma and not every traumatic event equates to PTSD.

We know officer involved incidents are going to happen, and there are fear inducing statistics regarding trauma as well as the potential result of PTSD, addiction, or suicide. The truth is that what might impact one person may not impact another. My husband sometimes trains other mental health professionals with me and tells them, "Not every incident is trauma and not every traumatic event equates to PTSD." There is a lot of information being put out there in regard to the mental health impact of the job (or maybe it's just my Instagram feed) and it can be quite scary. As a spouse, it can make us vigilant to the emotional state of our spouses. What isn't really talked about is that the majority of officers do *not* leave the job with PTSD. It's also not really mentioned that [3]spouses can be impacted as well. What isn't mentioned is the delayed onset that can occur with PTSD. I don't say all of this to scare you but normalize that this is our reality, and as a couple, we need to be aware of the potential impact and do our best to be proactive.

There are events that my husband is exposed to on a regular basis that would greatly have an adverse impact on most people. I like to say that what makes first responders heroes is the fact that they are humans doing extraordinary things. What seems to be a common thread for my husband and other first responders I speak to is the humanization of a situation. It's when they hear the cries of a loved one, see something familiar to them they connect with, or kids being injured. Kids are the hardest. I will talk more in the upcoming chapters about how to move through trauma and everyday resilience. While they are not all impacted the same way, they are all impacted. The human body cannot witness or be exposed to so many situations without having to modify or adjust in some way.

Most of us simply don't know how to support someone through pain.

Some departments incorporate critical incident debriefings after an event or even utilize peer support teams in order to assist officers in moving through an incident. As a spouse, we are often left out of any debriefings or "peer" support processes. I know that some departments have spouse support groups but in my experience they are rare. If you have been through a critical incident, you may know or understand this. Many times there is some support up front so it is on everyone's mind. People reach out to check on you and bring casseroles. Then, just like when someone passes away, the support dwindles. People go on with their lives. It's not out of malice. Most of us simply don't know how to support someone through pain.

The body adapts but is impacted by the chronic exposure to these situations and incidents. Most of us would not accept a job where we were required to receive a dose of poison on a daily basis. You would not be sure of the size of the dose you would receive that day, only that you would have to ingest it. You may notice small shifts in your digestive system, fatigue, or your ability to think clearly in situations. It doesn't seem to be difficult to swallow the poison and the amount on average seems small but, in actuality, it is slowly causing damage. I have also heard the analogy of cuts, small cuts that are annoying when you go to juice a lemon, but that you don't really notice. They are painful but not debilitating. Another example of this is the Boiling Frog theory in which a frog is placed in room temperature water on the stove. Ever so slowly, the water temperature is increased and the frog's body adjusts to the new temperature. This happens over and over until the water temperature is unbearable or boiling. Due to the frog's body continually adjusting, the frog's body does not sense the danger, and it dies. (Just a note that this is a fable and frogs will jump out.) The point being that the body adjusts and an officer may not realize they are in trouble mentally until their body can take no more. Every shift, officers figuratively ingest a dose of poison, they get a cut, or the temperature is slowly increased. The impact can be so delayed that the impact may not be recognized until retirement.

I don't write all this to scare or overwhelm you. I write this to hopefully normalize that we have a ***hell*** of a lot added into the mix of our relationship thanks to being a part of law enforcement. Sometimes people will mention how "tough it must be" to be married to an officer or to have a marriage in law enforcement and they mention not being around each other or say that dreaded phrase, "I don't know how you can do it." What they don't get and we sometimes forget is that there are so many aspects just on the surface of the relationship that we work through as a couple. These are the things that we can *see* in some respect. What people don't understand is that there are "no-see-ums" that most couples do not understand, that aren't explained to officers, and that wind up impacting marriage and relationships in negative ways.

THE UNDERPINNING

We were sitting in a deer blind on a ranch in the Hill Country of Texas but there wasn't much action at the time. One day was too warm and another day was too cold and most of the deer were bedded down. The ones that were walking around were young. Don't worry, no animals were harmed in this story. There was a lot of silence (because you don't talk much in a deer blind) which means that I was doing a lot of thinking.

Things were changing some in our relationship because I had started doing work on myself. I had started sharing more about me and dealing with some of my own "stuff" that I hadn't in the past. (Thank you Brené Brown!) My own "stuff" was impacting our relationship mostly because my coping skills of shutting down and shutting out were eroding. We had started to have real conversations about how him being in law enforcement impacted me and sucked at times. We had seen relationships and marriages end only to start new ones and see those end as well.

We had seen officers buy new cars every other year, boats, and ATVs, and wondered what we were doing wrong, only to realize they were in debt up to their ears. We had seen officers make poor decisions on duty, use the uniform to their advantage, and have affairs. We had seen substance related issues in officers and lost an officer to suicide using his service weapon while on substances. We had no idea what was going on but we were grateful it wasn't us. We had spent time fooling ourselves; we thought we were fine because we could not see those big problems and behaviors happening in our relationship.

We had started to have real conversations about how him being in law enforcement impacted me and sucked at times.

Yeah, we just had slow erosion and isolation (insert an eye roll here). I had been counseling officers in my practice and I saw these themes of behavior. In the silence of that cold morning, something shifted in me and I realized *something* has to be underneath all this. I wondered why and what caused a group of people that *say* they want to protect and serve to become complete assholes. Why could the public tell me how great my husband is and I think, "oh you have *no* idea what he says about you at home!"? Why can he hold it all together at work and then blow his top at home? Why am I getting all the shit? Why is this a pattern I'm hearing about in so many other relationships?

COOPER'S COLORS & OODA

My first clue happened when I was attending the Texas Counseling Association Conference. I was sitting in the front row because I was on the Board of Directors at the time, which meant I had to pay attention. We were listening to a combat veteran talk about PTSD. He was describing the fight or flight response which I was familiar with but started to add some aspects that occur during combat. To review, the fight or flight response is the (automated) process that happens in your brain when it anticipates danger.

It was super helpful when there were bears to run from but now gets triggered by kids screaming, traffic, the news, and anything else that your brain decides to interpret as a threat to your existence. More about that in a minute. Our keynote speaker was going into greater depth about the fight or flight response during combat. He explained that he wanted the fight or flight response to be intense because he needed to survive and respond.

If it becomes too intense, the body goes into "the black" which literally causes individuals to freeze in the middle of a combat situation and not be able to respond. He went on to explain this in more detail using "Cooper's Colors." He also went on to explain and teach us about John Boyd's OODA loop which stands for Observe, Orient, Decide, and Act. I remember hearing all of this and thinking, "Holy *shit*! This is exactly what my husband does when we leave the house!"

This was the moment I mentioned at the beginning when I so excitedly texted my husband and wrote, "Do you OODA?" Finding out these pieces of information blew the doors open when it came to understanding my husband and I was *so* excited. When I talk about the OODA loop to groups, they often have the same "ah-ha" moment as I experience them smiling, nodding, knowingly laughing, and spouses nudging their officers.

Cooper's Colors was developed by Lt Col. Jeff Cooper, a veteran from WWII and the Korean War, and written about in his book Principles of Self Defense. It is largely associated with the idea of a "combat mindset" and describes the state of one's mind and the ability to handle a given situation properly. It is largely associated with a state of readiness, fight or flight response, and is, well, color-coded.

Cooper described it this way:

- **White:** Unaware and unprepared. The only thing that will save you here is the incompetence of your attacker. When confronted a common response is something like, "How can this be happening?"

- **Yellow:** Relaxed Alert. There is no specific threat but one is prepared that there may be the possibility of something happening. There may be a reason that comes up during the day that would cause me to react and I may have to shoot. If someone is carrying a weapon, Cooper would say this is the recommended state to be in. This is the state that one is aware of their surroundings and keeping an eye out or eye on people they may not know or in environments that are unfamiliar.
- **Orange:** Specific Alert. Something is not quite right and on the radar. There is a state of readiness that causes the brain and body to react and recognize that if x happens then I may have to shoot or react.
- **Red:** Fight. The trigger from above has been tripped and you now need to shoot or take action.
- **Black:** At some point in time, the US Marine Corps added "Black" as a color which is a state in which panic or fear has taken over and an individual is immobilized.

Note: If you want to see a diagram of Cooper's Colors, there is one available at www.holdthelinebook.com

While I may not always be ready to shoot, I can relate to the colors and my fight or flight response. When I am in my office alone and most of the time with a client, I am in the white, and I would be dead if anything happened as I am pretty unaware. I go into the yellow when I leave out the back door of my office and look around for potential threats, especially when it is dark. If I see someone outside, in the dark, and their behavior seems off, my fight or flight increases, and I start making a plan. I've never gone beyond that point but I'm not sure if I would skip over red and go directly to black and freeze up.

Officers are trained to be in a state of readiness while on duty and that spills over onto their presence outside of the job. As a new wife, I thought it ridiculous that my husband wanted to take a weapon when we drove the 45 minutes into Dallas to go to dinner. I mean, he's not working! Come on! Turn it off! When we were on vacation one time, we got into a cab and my fight or flight was through the roof as it was one heck of a scary ride and the driver was none too kind. (Yes, this is before Uber!) I remember turning to my husband and telling him that I wish he would have been carrying. He assured me that he always has a plan.

OODA

Always having a plan brings me to the second part that I learned that day, which is the OODA loop. This syncs in with the states of Cooper's Colors. As a wife, the process can be super annoying and misinterpreted.

The OODA loop was developed by military strategist, Col. John Boyd and applied the concept to combat operations. The process involves constant information feedback loops. It sounds like a decision making process when it's broken down. You might realize that you use the same process for a variety of situations like decide what you are going to do or say next. This process is specifically lined out for safety and combat.

The components of the loop are:

- **Observe:** Observing is more than just seeing what is happening around you. It is observation and awareness of your own physical, environmental, and mental state. It can also involve observing moral dimensions. It might involve observing facial expressions and actions, behaviors, or situations. It is observing the largest context that you can consider.

- **Orient:** Orientation has been said to be the most important part of the loop. It takes what you are observing and puts it into context. This is where your environment becomes situational. So, while someone may be observing a facial expression your own personal bias or experience could impact the way you interpret the expression. It involves analysis at a high level. This analysis can be conscious, unconscious, or instinctual.
- **Decide:** Having gathered information that is needed, a decision is made. The previous steps have gathered a great deal of information and based upon the information, the most relevant or effective decision is made. Boyd cautions that one cannot make the same decision over and over without evaluation.
- **Act:** Take action. The process is a continual loop which may result in an individual staying in the mental process of observe, orient, and decide over and over and over.

This process keeps an individual mentally prepared to take action and on top of a situation. It is also exhausting.

Note: You can check out a visual depiction of the OODA loop at www.holdthelinebook.com

How many times have you gone into a restaurant and known exactly where you are going to sit? Yup, a corner of the restaurant with the back against the wall.

Admittedly, these states of readiness keep officers safe and I would not want it any other way. It becomes integrated into an officer's brain and becomes instinctual due to their conditioning.

How many times have you gone into a restaurant and known exactly where you are going to sit? Yup, a corner of the restaurant with the back against the wall. As spouses we laugh about it and roll our eyes many times. We accommodate it and make sure that our officer is comfortable with their positioning.

What can even be funnier is going out with a police couple and watching the officers trying to decide who will have the most strategic position. Spouses get it. When I was first married, I had no idea why this was actually a "thing". After I learned about the OODA loop and Cooper's Colors, I started to understand there was an actual reason for the choice.

There were many times when we went out that I thought my husband just didn't care about what I was saying. We would be out and about and I would be talking or discussing something with him. What I observed is that he was looking around the room sometimes with his eyes and sometimes with his head swiveling. My interpretation of this? He wasn't interested in or listening to what I was saying. I was taught that when you are speaking to someone, you look them in the eyes. That wasn't happening. I would often just stop talking or say things like, "Never mind. You're not listening." Sometimes he would tell me that he was listening and other times he would just say, "ok." It built resentment between us. There were other times when I would try to figure out what he was looking at and if it was another woman. I would give him a hard time about who he was, "checking out." I have worked with couples that had major arguments about the officer not paying attention or checking out other women and not admitting to it. Being in the "Yellow" and the OODA loop can cause us as a couple to build resentment and shut down on one another when in actuality, it's just a conditioned loop and state that the officer is sometimes not even aware of to share with the spouse. When I have talked about the OODA loop, some officers are not even aware that the process has a name.

Knowing this changed our interaction. My favorite story to tell about this shift for us was when we went into the bank one day to make a deposit. We were running errands and I had a lot of cash that had been collected from my office. I was just going to run in and make the deposit, but my husband decided to go as well, of course. He wanted to make sure I was safe. I get that. So, we go into the building and have to wait in line which is in the middle of the building. I'm chatting away talking about who knows what. I turn to look at him and he places his body in that "comfortable cop" stance and I see him looking around and then every now and then slowly turning his body. He is responding to me but doing his thing. I just start laughing. He suddenly turns to me and says, "What?!" I told him that he was doing his OODA thing. He smirked and admitted that was exactly what was going on in his brain. I then asked him about everything that he was observing and orienting to and what decisions he would make if he needed to take action. It was very entertaining.

Knowing what is going on when his head is swiveling, or his eyes are looking around has really helped our relationship. I'll check in with him to make sure he is listening or if I need to pause. He has learned to give me some more feedback than just "uh huh" to ensure that he is actually hearing me.

The OODA loop process also interferes with our vacations or other activities at times. Since this process is conditioned into their brain, it doesn't necessarily stop when they are on vacation, decide to go shopping during the holidays, or a concert. Before I understood all this, I would say, "Can't you just relax and enjoy yourself? Geesh!" I would be so frustrated because it felt like he wasn't there with me enjoying the experience. He was just.....there. I still get frustrated at times but now that frustration comes with a little sadness that he cannot turn it off in the way that I can. I won't say that I'm a "sheep," but I do not observe half of what he does.

Many times, we pick vacation spots that don't include crowds. We like to go to small towns or countryside locations. We both find them relaxing. But, there are times when you are traveling that you really have to go do the touristy things that include crowds. When we were in Italy one year visiting my college roommate, we went to Florence with her and her sister who was also visiting. My friend was showing us around as she had been there before. At one point in time, she took us down a side street and I could actually feel my husband's body stiffen up. I looked at him and I asked if he was ok. He just gave me a look. He wasn't. I saw him go into more of an 'Orange' state as we were stopped right in front of a bus station with some people that looked at us like we might be targets. I could see him in a high alert but trying to let my friend reorient herself. He calmly leaned over and whispered to me to please get us off the street quickly and back onto the main roads. I suggested that we head to a coffee shop (which are everywhere) and talk about where we needed to go from there.

My husband appreciated me taking the lead on that. There were several times that day where I could tell that he felt overwhelmed with his own processes and trying to keep an eye on where my friend and her sister were. I would take time and come up with a plan with them instead of it feeling like chaos for him. When we got off the train and back to the house, he thanked me for helping out and understanding what was going on with him.

Prior to understanding the OODA and Cooper's Colors, the trip into Florence would have been very different. He would have made requests of me that I thought were ridiculous. He would have become agitated, frustrated, and anxious as I remained unaware of my surroundings just doing my own thing. I would have thought he was being a controlling asshole, irritated with me or the situation, or felt anxious and on eggshells waiting for him to blow up. Sometimes I would just shut down and pout or act out in some way. It would have ended up in some kind of argument about him trying to dictate what we were doing and never being able to just relax and have fun. I remember many times in situations like these telling him to just "turn it off". He could never explain what was going on, just that the need to have control in situations like that intensified when he felt like he didn't have control. What we recognized was that he was being flooded with information, constantly orienting, and trying to decide, but as the environment moved and changed so quickly, his fight or flight response was increasing.

When we do fail, we have become better with quickly recognizing what is happening and recovering with each other.

Working within the system was important to us so we talked about how to accommodate the process but not let it control. I still wander into stores and look around. What's different is that I make a plan and act a little less spontaneously. I tell him that I want to go into store x and y and place of interest z. He can then decide where he wants to stand, where he wants to go, or if he has concerns. We check in with each other a lot when we travel in crowded places. Having a break in a coffee shop has been a way that he can tone down the process for a while in order to feel better when we jump back into the crowd. We talk about things that make him feel safer like, sadly, not holding my hand at times or him holding on to my passport or the way I am carrying my handbag. He owns up when he is feeling overwhelmed, so he doesn't get angry with me. Neither of us is perfect with our process. When we do fail, we have become better with quickly recognizing what is happening and recovering with each other.

This is a good time for me to point something out. Officers are impacted and conditioned in certain ways by their job. It is important as a couple to work to navigate through them. It is not the spouse's job to accommodate over and over again and excuse the behavior. That is called enabling. Spouses can offer a generous explanation of the behavior. It is the officer's job to work to navigate through the conditioned behavior so it does not impact the relationship or family.

HYPERVIGILANCE

There are times that I watch my husband get ready for work, and after 20 years I can see when his mind starts getting ready for work as well. I used to joke with him and say if anyone ever wanted to kill him, they simply needed to know what time he needed to be on duty and plan backward about 2 hours. He had a routine doing the same things in the same way in the same order any day that he went to work. I now can recognize that routine is a ritual for him. It is a ritual for him to not only get his physical self ready for work, but his mind starts to get ready for work. Early on I would try to talk to him when he was getting ready and found that it didn't work very well. I also found that talking to him after work didn't work very well. I would get those minimal responses like, "uh huh," "sure," "right," "ok," or sometimes nothing. It was annoying as we really didn't see each other due to shifts and working.

Spouses would tell me about how their officer would just sit in the recliner all day, flip channels without really watching anything, mindlessly play video games for hours on end, scroll on their phone without really reading anything, and the complaint that their officer just wasn't engaged with them or the kids when he was home. It kind of seemed they were just mindlessly existing on at least the first day off and then sometimes there was a shift on the second day. There was talk about wanting to have conversation with them and also getting the minimal responses or like they were half-listening. As wives, we would talk about how annoying it was, but we just figured they were tired. Maybe you experience this as an officer or as a spouse and you know what I'm talking about.

The real reason for this behavior is hypervigilance. As a counselor, I learned about hypervigilance as an alert state of arousal due to a triggering event or situation usually associated with trauma. I never associated it as something that officers experience daily; however, that is exactly what is happening to officers when they go on the job. Oftentimes as humans, we are vigilant when we are driving, crossing a street, watching kids on the playground, or in numerous other situations. Vigilance is a state of readiness in case we need to make a quick maneuver if a car comes into our lane, jump out of the way of a car, or run to kids if they get into a dangerous situation. While our body is aware and prepared, it is not in a state of high arousal. Hypervigilance is a heightened state of sensory arousal which allows officers to be acutely aware of the behavior and is accompanied by greater behavioral response.

Dr. Gilmartin in his book Emotional Survival for Law Enforcement explains this state and the impact of the state. I strongly recommend that as an officer or spouse you read the book. Hypervigilance is a biological process involving a dance (and sometimes a fight) of sorts between the limbic system, the complex system concerning instinct and mood, and the pre-frontal cortex where decisions are made. When an officer goes on patrol, their brain usually goes into this heightened state of arousal. [1]Gilmartin states that, "Hypervigilance is the necessary manner of viewing the world from a threat-based perspective, having the mindset to see the events unfolding as potentially hazardous." Hypervigilance is not a mindset; it is a biological process. Hypervigilance is not a mindset; it is a biological process.

You are probably very aware of the term "fight or flight". It is helpful to know a little about the biological functions that happen as a part of the response. I don't share this to bore you but so you can understand that officers are impacted by their biological system and thus, have to work to overcome or sometimes have the inability to overcome biological processes. First, let's talk about the HPA axis which is short for Hypothalamus, Pituitary, and Adrenal. The HPA axis works like this: the hypothalamus receives information that stuff is about to get intense, it then signals the pituitary gland, and pituitary gland signals the adrenal gland. There are then neurotransmitters, like dopamine, epinephrine (adrenaline), and norepinephrine, are released as well as cortisol Adrenaline is the stuff that prepares the body for fight or flight. It makes you better, faster, and stronger. It prepares you to react in a variety of ways to a threat. It also takes a great deal of energy and wears you out faster than normal. Enter cortisol which is the hormone that stimulates the liver to elevate your blood sugar and the metabolism of fats and protein that create the energy you need. Cortisol is released into our body's system, which causes a response by the [2]automated nervous system including increased blood pressure, pulse, respiration, and body temperature. It also causes eyes to dilate and increases peripheral vision, improves hearing, increases reflex and reaction responses, and increases blood sugar production. Gilmartin quotes an officer in his [3]book saying, "I get that alive, high-energy, quick-thinking feeling that makes the reds redder and the blues bluer." Everything is more alive and more stimulating for the officer. Often officers will feel more clever and funny on the job versus when they are at home. This process in the brain helps the brain to make quick interpretations, decisions, and responses. It is what keeps officers safe and keeps them alive.

However, what goes up must come down. When an officer goes off duty, the processes start to reverse to recover from the alert state. The body must biologically recover from the process, and the "alive" state that the officer feels changes to withdrawal, detachment, isolation, and apathy. The prefrontal cortex, your brain's decision making center which assists with attention, impulse control, and judgement, is exhausted and goes off line. While we cannot all relate to the process of hypervigilance, we can most certainly relate to the "come down" effect of our bodies being stimulated. Our bodies and brains do not know the difference of arousal from a positive event or negative event; it is just aroused. You may be able to recall a positive event that was exciting and then feeling completely exhausted at the end and need to just "veg out." While it is not exactly the impact, it is similar, and officers go through this every day they are on duty. And the recovery period for this effect? 18 to 24 hours. Meaning, officers are not usually able to recover fully before they have to go back on duty and do the cycle all over again. This is why spouses and families often feel their officer is disengaged when they come home.

Note: You can see the ups and downs of the hypervigilance cycle at www.holdthelinebook.com

When couples are unaware of the process of hypervigilance, there are frustrations and miscommunications. The officer's lack of ability to engage or make decisions is interpreted as disinterest and often personalized by spouses, thinking they have done something wrong or that their spouse is not in love with them. This can set up a cycle within the relationship. Spouses sometimes resort to complaining in order to push their officer to get off the couch and help with the kids, housework, or to just talk. The officer then starts to blame the spouse for being a nag and the officer's brain starts to interpret home as negative space. They incorrectly interpret that they must be unhappy at home because they feel so alive and energetic at work. The officer then may start making decisions based upon this assumption leading to behaviors such as irritation, isolation, emotional disengagement, avoidance of being home, or affairs.

Officers, spouses, and families lose in the hypervigilance cycle. The biological process of the coming down interrupts engagement with not only spouses but with their kids. Spouses and children already miss so much of their officer with shift work and they miss out on even more in the recovery period. Officers lose out as their life can start to slip away, not only missing out on interactions and relationships with their family but also the ability to interact with their friends and their hobbies. Gilmartin refers to a [4]concept of the "usta" syndrome in which officers slowly lose elements of their life they had prior to policing such as hobbies and interests. I asked a client one time what he did in his free time when he was off duty. He told me fishing and I inquired about the last time he went fishing and what he had caught if anything. He thought about it a long time and then said something to the effect of, "Holy Cow. It's probably been 3-4 years since I went." That, folks, is the "usta" syndrome.

Another effect or impact of hypervigilance is the "sparkly object syndrome." When I hear people speaking about sparkly object syndrome, I often hear people talk about becoming distracted from their focus. I call these my "squirrel moments." It is also used when people get excited about a new concept or activity and dive headfirst into something, often abandoning something else and/or leaving things undone. In this case, I am using the phrase to refer to the biological process of the brain wanting to get a "hit." While there are several chemicals in our brain, the one that is often associated with it is dopamine. It's the reason people make goals and resolutions. It's the reason that you might buy something only to think later, "What was I thinking?"

Earlier I mentioned that the officer inaccurately projects being down and depressed at home, on the family or spouse rather than understanding there is a biological process occurring. The brain is saying, "Home bad. Find other ways to be happy." When in actuality, the brain is wanting to be stimulated in the way it is stimulated on the job. Just like the neurotransmitters we discussed earlier, epinephrine and cortisol that shows up in the alert hypervigilant state, dopamine is one of the main neurotransmitters the brain creates in a pleasure state. It's a big part of our unique human ability to plan and think, and helps us to focus, strive and find things interesting. And just like the alert version of hypervigilance, it becomes habituated, something sought after. It is also a "high" state

The brain starts looking for ways to get the dopamine hit and when it finds it, the officer's behavior may start to be driven by the need for the hit. I hear officers joke about the guy in the department that is always buying a new vehicle, boat, ATV, etc. What is not a joke is that many officers overextend themselves financially justifying it by working overtime. This pattern of behavior just increases the impact of hypervigilance and the negative impact on them and the family. The "hits" can also come in the form of video games, social media, and texting with people at work about stimulating calls. It can also come from messaging "badge bunnies" on social media, drinking, porn, gambling, or a variety of other activities.

I once had an officer that contacted me over social media. He told me he loved his wife and the life he had and could not understand why he was on the verge of meeting up with a girl that kept messaging him. He didn't want to, yet, he wanted to. I explained that his brain found it exciting and was motivating his behavior. I also told him that if he did love his wife and his life, he needed to understand how the cycle of hypervigilance was impacting his decision-making process and what to do to re-engage with his life instead of letting his primal brain run the show.

MINDSET

Our brains are shaped a lot by our experiences. Those experiences can be things that have happened to you personally or people you care about. These experiences change the way we see the world and what is happening. They also influence our brain giving it cues on what to filter in, and what to filter out.

Our brains are wired for survival. The only goal of the brain is to keep us alive. It is there to keep us safe and protect us. It is not there to make us happy. The keeping happy part or finding joy, that takes work. A lot of work! In fact, the human brain is actually pretty lazy. Anyone who longs for an afternoon nap knows that conserving energy is essential for human survival. Prehistoric humans required efficiency for the search for food, shelter, competing for sexual partners, and avoiding predators. So our efficient brain develops patterns, habits.

When I first met my husband, the way he drove made me a little crazy. We drove very differently. He actually drove the SPEED LIMIT! I remember visiting him and riding with him on the highway in Baltimore and thinking he was so very calm as a driver. I, on the other hand, like speed. This might partly be because many of the highways in Texas are 70 mph and sometimes that feels like a suggestion. When he moved down to Texas, I took the last leg of the journey which included a 2-lane state highway that had quite a few curves with a speed limit of 70. I remember I was driving probably 75-78 and would pass people as I needed to. He was slightly nervous. Hey! We are a big state and we have places to get! Fast forward several years later, my well-mannered speed limit following husband is now cussing at people for going slow, being in his way, and telling me that they all need tickets for DWHUA! (That would be Driving with Head Up Ass.) What really gets me riled up is when he starts flipping people off. I yell at him to stop because, in Texas, people can get shot for that. Now, I am the nervous one, my fight or flight response reacting and going through the roof, either telling him to "calm down" or just plotting how I can never ride with him again. (By the way, if people could "calm down", they would. When a person's fight or flight is triggered, telling them to "calm down" will be seen as an attack which will just make you the target.) So, how did we get from a mild-mannered driver to aggressive?

Habits get formed that are both positive and negative. The more negative we see in the world, the more the brain will think the world is a negative place. The more it thinks that the world is a negative dangerous place, the more the limbic part of your brain will be on high alert in a fight, flight, freeze, fawn state. The limbic part of the brain is a very primitive part of our brain system. It is where the survival instinct comes from. Only now, instead of bears, we have dangers like traffic, social media trolls, and work situations. Fight and flight are common to this response, either fighting or running away physically or mentally. Freeze is a little less familiar and is the inability to respond. You will see this happen in children when they are presented with a choice and do not want to choose either. You may have felt this when you were confronted with something and found you just couldn't respond, you find yourself staring and not knowing what to do. Fawn is even less familiar. It is a people-pleasing behavior and is an attempt by the brain to smooth out the situation quickly. For this Southern girl, it means my voice goes up about an octave and I say something or behave in a way that is really not congruent with what I am wanting to do or thinking.

As I mentioned, our brains are wired for survival, and that means keeping you alive; the brain filters in any situation that, in the brain's opinion, *could* be a threat. The brain filters in what you are seeing, hearing, smelling, and tasting and interprets it through what it has learned about life. All of our brains are different because of our different experiences. What one person's brain may interpret as danger may not be another person's interpretation of danger. You can think of this as a lens that you and/or your brain sees the world through. If you have lived a life that has been relatively peaceful and kind, your lens or filter might not be as acute as someone who has lived through being bullied, abused, or some other type of danger. It impacts not only the way you see the world but how you respond to the world. It is actually difficult for *all* of us to see situations or the world in a positive way. The brain is going to naturally filter in the negative and if you are not aware, the lens you see the world through will become dark and cloudy. As an officer, your lens becomes very different. Remember my story above about driving? The lens became a negative mental filter as a consequence from interacting with the public on the job (everyone is an asshole) and the overactivation of the fight or flight response, also a consequence of the job. Mental filters and fight or flight.

THE SHEEPDOG

Law enforcement is responsible for responding to calls that, most of the time, involve an emergency or danger or at least have that potential. They take care of the public and watch for situations that could be a potential danger or crime (OODA loop). Based on their experiences, officers filter in situations that the unobservant public does not see. They see the people acting in ways that could make them targets for crime. People walking around staring at their phones, not being observant of their surroundings, or how they are interacting or not interacting with the world around them. The first time my husband told me that he didn't want me to be a "sheep," I was offended. I saw it as a negative way to see the world, like a really warped lens. Then I started to understand.

I used to watch Bugs Bunny and there was a cartoon where the Sheepdog and Wile E Coyote clocked in. The Sheepdog would go up on the hill and look down on the sheep, watching over them. Wile E Coyote on the other hand would go down in the meadow and try his various tricks in order to capture the sheep. Time and time again, Coyote would be foiled due to the Sheepdog being one step ahead by being able to predict what was going to happen. They would clock out at the end of the shift, the Sheepdog looking the same as he did when he walked in and Wile E Coyote clocking out battered, bruised, and broken. That is how officers see the world, except their brain does not clock out and neither does the mindset. It's perhaps a negative view, but also a realistic view for them.

I look back and I now understand his reaction to some of my behavior at times. That doesn't mean it doesn't suck, it just means that I get it. I had my iPhone stolen one day from my office. We had a typical medical type office with a waiting room and a door that separated the waiting room from the clinical offices. I would commonly leave my phone on top of a filing cabinet in the administrative/front desk area that was behind the waiting room door. We did not have a front desk person so when I was in session, no one was observing the waiting room or office. I came out of session one day and I couldn't find my phone anywhere. Within about 5 minutes, I figured out what happened. Of course, the police said they could take a report, but I knew they were not going to use their resources to find my phone. I called my husband and told him. His response was not one of compassion but instead something like, "I told you to lock that door. What did you expect?!?!" I was upset and concerned about my phone. He was probably thinking about all the other horrible things that could have happened because I didn't have the door locked. I was a victim that didn't take proper precautions. I was as a sheep.

CYNICISM

When you deal with the negative all day, you see things in a negative light. When you are consistently putting yourself in a potentially dangerous situation, your brain is going to predict the negative in order to protect you. Officers come in contact with two types of people all day long, victims and suspects.

There have been times when we have been driving and my husband will have a negative comment about someone just walking down the street, some negative inference that he has made by looking at the individual. My retort is almost always to spin it on him in some way. We do it in fun now, but in the past, it would lead to arguments.

For example, if there is a homeless person on the street asking for money, his assumption is that the person is using the money for drugs or is scamming people. I then think of an elaborate story of how the person lost their job, their housing, and their vehicle, and now they are just trying to get to Kansas.

Things are not always as they appear. When your job involves people being untruthful to get out of a situation or to hide something, it becomes your reality. Everyone you pull over that has been drinking just had two. There were ten people on a scene, but no one saw anything. Someone shoplifted, but has no idea how that item got in their purse. Officers naturally believe that everyone is lying. Makes sense.

Skepticism and cynicism get built into thinking, and this thinking helps to keep them safe.

Officers work within the premise that the majority of people are untrustworthy, deceptive, and hiding something. Officers are not going to trust. Skepticism and cynicism get built into thinking, and this thinking helps to keep them safe. Everyone's behavior and motives for those behaviors are up for interpretation and scrutiny. The more cynical an officer becomes, the more bullshit there is in the world, and the more assholes there are in the world causing it.

For a long while, I got frustrated at how my husband saw the world and worked to try to convince him it was different. I would have conversations with him about what was going on at work or with a group of neighbors, and he would consistently dismiss my comments with his own comments like, "well, that's just bullshit" or "don't listen to that asshole." That would be his whole comment. I would get frustrated because, bullshit or not, I had to deal with it and I couldn't just dismiss the situation like he was trying to. At times it was comical because I started to predict his response. At the same time, it wasn't comical, felt dismissive toward my experience or story, and was causing further disconnection and shut down in our relationship. Enter in again Dr. Gilmartin. I remember being at a hotel laying out by the pool, and coming to his [5]section on assholes and bullshit. I literally laughed so loud my friends jumped and asked what the hell was so funny. I took pictures and texted them to my husband. It was another one of those moments where I realized this was a part of the puzzle that neither of us understood, nor was it previously explained.

Gilmartin discusses the use of these two terms within the community. Remember that officers are dealing with one of two types of people: victims or suspects. They are having to respond to these individuals (the assholes), and the situations being caused (the bullshit). Officers and their brains need a way to displace what is going on, and calling things bullshit and the people that cause them assholes is something that allows them to keep doing what they are doing every day. This is called displacement. Displacement is a defense mechanism in which our brain redirects a negative emotion from the source to something less threatening. The discomfort that is caused by a person is displaced to the category of asshole. The discomfort that is caused by the event is displaced to the category of bullshit. This is a way that their brain keeps them safe. The alternative is for the brain to absorb all the incidents it is exposed to and see the world as a dangerous place, which would cause anxiety to the point of paralysis. This mindset carries them through and then bleeds over into other aspects and relationships in their life.

SPILLOVER

It's 11 PM and I've stayed up waiting for my officer husband to come home. He walks in the door, says hello to me, and gives me a kiss. I go back to the couch finishing the show I'm watching. He looks at the kitchen, gives a deep sigh, and picks up a sponge. Mind you he is still in uniform with his duty belt on. There are also no dishes in the sink, nor food on the counter. Yet, he is cleaning the counter tops, lifting up burners, slamming them down, and grumbling about the G.D. crumbs on the counter. In my mind, I think that I must have really screwed up cleaning up somehow and I'll do better tomorrow.

There is some history here that you need to know. In my house growing up, my brother and I would clean up the kitchen after dinner, but it was no big deal if there were dessert or evening snack dishes in the sink. My husband grew up in a house that was very clean, especially the kitchen. My husband also worked in the restaurant industry for 15 years before he decided to become an officer. He is slightly obsessive when it comes to chicken juice! I know he likes a clean kitchen and appreciates not getting salmonella. This behavior was new and a little irritating, as I had just made myself a little dinner.

The next night I make sure that I get all the crumbs off the counter before I relax. My husband comes home and has more of the same behavior. This goes on for years. Sometimes he swears about the GD crumbs, the streaks on the stove, the handle being sticky on the refrigerator, or some other minor thing. Because he is on shifts, sometimes I see the behavior and sometimes I hear it when he comes home. I go from thinking that I can do better at cleaning up the kitchen, to feeling criticized, to feeling resentful as hell and thinking, "F off dude!" in my mind.

One day, probably five years later, when he is cleaning the kitchen in uniform, after going to some couples counseling training (lol), I say, "The story that I have is that you think I cannot ever clean the kitchen good enough for you." He stops, looks at me with his kind eyes, and says, "this has nothing to do with you." I think he was sad to know that I thought that for five years. For five years I thought I wasn't good enough, and it had been a wedge in our relationship. He went on to tell me, "I feel so powerless and out of control when I come home from work. Everyone tells me what to do all day long. It is just cleaning up shit all day long and it never ends. When I come home, I want to feel like I have some control. I come home and wiping down the counter helps me to settle down a little bit and feel like there is something I can have control of. I do it and I feel satisfied." I asked him about the swearing about stuff in the kitchen not being clean. He told me, "I do that to let off some steam. I can be aggravated at the damn crumbs or streaks or spot on the counter and then I don't take it out on you or the dogs." I never knew. I was feeling his anger, irritation, annoyance, and frustration, and built up my own contempt toward him. He thought he was sparing me from the spillover.

I didn't call it spillover at the time. What I did know is that this police crap seemed to come in his mindset, tone, and in other ways that I didn't really get or understand. I found it annoying. Sometimes it caused me to lose respect for him, and other times caused me to shut down. Most of all, it was infecting our relationship. There came the day when I received one of my counseling research journals in the mail. I know, nerd. As I scanned it, I found an [1]article about law enforcement and spillover. BAM! Just like that I had another puzzle piece to help our relationship.

The concept of spillover is exactly what it sounds like. Aspects of one life spills over onto another aspect of life. It sounds so simple when you think in terms of non-first responder jobs, right? I have an emotionally difficult case and I'm feeling drained. There is a deadline to meet at work and I'm feeling pressured. There is a person at work causing drama and I wonder how it's going to impact me. It can even spillover to extended family, health concerns, children, and grief. The list can go on and on. There is a different kind of spillover with first responders, and in our case law enforcement. The job doesn't just stop when they get off duty. As an officer or a spouse, you know that there is impact psychologically and biologically. You cannot do the job without there being change. If you are not aware of how it is changing you, it oozes out of your pores and on to your spouse, children, and other relationships. It can take control and drive your behavior and beliefs in a direction far away from the person you want to be. The spillover is toxic.

> ***The job doesn't just stop when they get off duty.***

When I talk to people over social media or the LE couples, they don't recognize that what is happening in their relationship is a part of spillover. I didn't recognize it for years! Spillover results in disconnection, lack of motivation, anxiety, depression, anger, communication problems, apathy, lack of empathy, callousness, numbing, problems with intimacy and sex (because they are different), and many other issues. The spillover can escalate to problems with alcohol, porn, addiction, affairs, over eating, over exercising, and abuse. This is not a complete list, but rather things that are spilling out of my head as I write. Just because the spillover *can* result in these things does not mean it is the sole issue. Just because there is spillover from the job does not mean the behavior is justified and spouses need to suck it up and live with it. As a law enforcement couple, we *both* need to be aware of the potential of spillover, and then adjust.

JUST TURN IT OFF

I mentioned before that I really wanted my husband to just turn it off. I have a process I go through when I get off to shed what I can as I drive the 20 minutes home. Most days I'm successful. Some days I'm not. I didn't understand what made this so hard for my husband. There were, and are, times when I tell my husband, "I'm not one of your citizens!" or "This isn't a scene you need to control." There are also those moments when my husband gets "the look" of intensity and intimidation or uses his authority voice in that snappy, short, staccato way. There are the emotional reactions to situations or events that seem larger than necessary. I just wanted him to shed all of that, take off the uniform, and get back into his fun, silly, caring self.

Officers are conditioned to react, not respond.

My belief was that he was choosing to act this way because he liked the power or control he felt at work. The more I took time to look at the research, read blogs, and talk to officers and wives, the more I realized I was not unique in this experience and there were psychological reasons for the behavior. Officers are conditioned to react, not respond.

REACTING VS. RESPONDING

Our brain is wired for survival and to protect us from danger. The part of the brain that is responsible for this task is the amygdala. Its job is to scan for this danger and react accordingly, either fight, flight, freeze, or fawn. The amygdala is the only part of the brain that is fully formed at birth and is completely functional. It stores your emotional memories, and it does not have a filter, so it keeps all of the good stuff and all of the bad stuff. It is also really good at building roads to really important memories. These roads are called neural pathways and they are built when a particular memory has special meaning. The more meaning, the better the road. There are definitely times when we want the amygdala to take over.

Let's use driving as an example. When you were learning how to drive, you were probably nervous, awkward, made some dumb decisions at first or were overly cautious. I still remember the first time my driving instructor told me we were getting on the highway! I was scared!

You probably do a lot of things differently now compared to when you were first learning to drive. Heck, maybe you get in the car to go somewhere and don't even remember the drive to get there. Or, maybe you're like me and find yourself exiting at your work exit rather than the exit to go to the grocery store. Or how about this one, you change jobs and find yourself driving to your old office one day when you aren't paying attention. Your brain is doing a lot based upon what it has been conditioned to do. You have trained it. It is a habit. And, like a memory in your amygdala, a habit is very much the same thing, a neural pathway. So, if you are sitting at your old office parking lot reading this book, you have a strong habit formed.

Your brain also learns along the way, then takes that information and causes your body to react. When someone cuts you off in traffic or pulls out in front of you, you don't say to yourself, "I'm going to slam on my brake and jerk the wheel to the left." You just do it. Your brain takes over. There are also the times when you see someone and think, "That person is totally going to cut me off." And they do! Are you a mind reader? No! Your brain is picking up on something and preparing you to react in a situation. Our brain learns as it goes along in life and decides appropriate reactions to protect and keep us safe while accomplishing what we need to accomplish. If it didn't do that, none of us would drive.

I spend a lot of time in the therapy room working with people teaching them how to manage their fight or flight response, often by-passing that pesky amygdala, and moving into their prefrontal cortex (also called the frontal lobe) which helps them to make decisions. This is the part of the brain that we want to inhabit the most. The prefrontal cortex is the last part of the brain to develop and it is responsible for helping us achieve and set goals. It receives input from a number of regions throughout the brain to process information and adapts accordingly. Like the captain of a sports team or the conductor of an orchestra, it acts as the executive director of the brain. When I am with my clients, I am working with them to stop reacting and start responding. The whole point is to slow the reaction which is usually based upon a fear response and does not get us to the place we want to be.

For example, if someone cuts you off in traffic, a reaction would be to give them the middle finger salute. Another emotional reaction would be to run them off the road, or on the flip side, need to suddenly get to the side of the road and stop a panic attack. Our brain interprets a threat and we react. It gets people in trouble in relationships, on the job, and sometimes can lead to legal problems.

As helpful as that amygdala is, we have to know when and how to override the reaction. When we work to respond to a situation, we take a moment, sometimes an audible breath or sigh, and then respond utilizing our frontal lobe or decision part of our brain. Now when someone cuts us off in traffic, we may startle but then sigh and back off. (Hey, I'm thinking of an ideal here!)

> ***When we work to respond to a situation, we take a moment, sometimes an audible breath or sigh, and then respond utilizing our frontal lobe or decision part of our brain.***

While this skill and brain function are something helpful in almost all workplaces, not only would I not want officers to go through this process on the job day in and day out, their hypervigilance response is working against them. I want them conditioned to react. I want their fight or flight to kick in along with their training and act. It keeps them safe. I just don't want that at home, with me, or our family.

CONDITIONING

First responders are conditioned to react. They are told to go from call to call to call. They hear dispatch and they go. In that moment, there is another dump of cortisol and nuerotransmitters and their body biologically reacts. There is not a minute to think, "mmmmmm do I have all my gear? Do I need to go to the bathroom before I head out on this call?" They just jump and go. This is a conditioned response to react. If officers are at a scene and a situation escalates, officers do not pause to think about the course of action. Their training kicks in and their body takes over. This is the same, thank goodness, for many professionals. We condition our brain to react certain ways in certain situations.

If you took Psychology 101, you may remember the term conditioning. You may even remember Pavlov's Dog. Here's the story. This guy, Pavlov, had a dog named Bierka. He actually had a lot of dogs, but Bierka is the most famous. Anyway, Pavlov was studying salivation in dogs (bleck!) and had a small tube in their mouth that recorded the saliva when the dogs were fed. What he started noticing was that the dogs would start salivating when they heard the footsteps of the assistant coming to feed them. The food did not have to be present for the reaction of salivation to start. The dog's brain had become conditioned to respond to the footsteps instead of food. The stimulus and the reward have to be present very close together for the brain to start to become conditioned. Pavlov later tried this with a bell with the same results. He rang the bell and presented the dog with food. Eventually, he would ring the bell and the dog would start to salivate, even if he was not presented with food. This form of conditioning is called classical conditioning.

A good example of classical conditioning is the alarm or "tones" that go off before firefighters get called out from the station. Almost every firefighter and paramedic will tell me that their body reacts to the "click" from the P.A. system, rather than the alarm or tone itself. They know this because when they go home and their refrigerator "clicks" on, they tell me about their reaction. Some will be in a dead sleep, hear the refrigerator click, wake up, and then take a while to get back to sleep due to their body reacting. In law enforcement, this could be called the flinch or startle response.

Conditioning is also formed from the learning that comes from trial and error experiences. This is called operant conditioning. This is the type of conditioning that is used in parenting; it often involves reinforcement, which is considered encouraging a behavior, and punishment, which is considered discouraging a behavior. This can either be positive (adding something) or negative (removing something). Here's what you need to know about reinforcement and punishment:

- Positive Reinforcement: The behavior is reinforced by adding something positive.
- Negative Reinforcement: The behavior is reinforced by removal of a negative.
- Positive Punishment: The behavior is reinforced by adding an undesirable consequence.
- Negative Punishment: The behavior is reinforced by removing something.

You're probably thinking, "OMG Cyndi! You are a nerd and I don't know where all this is going." Stick with me. One of my first podcasts was about operant conditioning and there is a reason why.

Let me give you an example first.

Hank has a really messy room and you want Hank to be neater.

Here are your options:

- Positive Reinforcement: Hank cleans up his room and receives ice cream and love. (Tidy is reinforced with a reward.)
- Negative Reinforcement: Hank cleans up his room and avoids the nagging that comes if he does not. (Tidy is reinforced by lack of negative.)
- Positive Punishment: Hank decides not to clean his room and now has to clean the bathroom as well. (Messy is discouraged by having to do more.)
- Negative Punishment: Hank decided not to clean his room and his tech time is taken away for the next day (Messy is discouraged by taking something away.)

Let's take this from a law enforcement perspective while on the job. An officer comes on a scene and needs to get control of a suspect. Here are the officer choices and possible consequences.

- Positive Reinforcement: Officer acts with authority and people comply or situations de-escalate.
- Negative Reinforcement: Officer acts with authority which avoids an escalation.
- Positive Punishment: Office does not act with authority and has to go to class.
- Negative Punishment: Officer does not act with authority and is written up or injured.

Classical conditioning is helpful to know. Operant conditioning is essential to understand because it impacts both the officer, spouse, and the family. It is a major part of eggshells being created within relationships. Officers are conditioned to get control of a scene and assert authority. They learn to do this with their posture, facial expressions, voices, and if necessary, physically. The brain becomes conditioned to have control or to react in certain ways when there is the potential for chaos or lack of control.

CONDITIONING IN RELATIONSHIPS

As I mentioned, one of the first podcasts I published was about conditioning. It's actually episode two. That tells you how important I think it is that we understand how we can become conditioned in our relationship. In the podcast episode, I tell the story about my brother taking me to a U2 concert. (An amazing experience if you grew up with U2 like I did. I mean we were *feet* away from the stage!)

I was really excited to be going with my brother and nephew; however about lunch time, I found out my husband's shift changed from ending at 10 p.m. to 6 p.m. My automatic conditioned response was an overwhelming sense that I should stay home and not go to the concert. This is how powerful conditioning is, and a great example of how I had become conditioned. Over the years, my brain had strung together that if my husband was off duty and we *could* be together, we *should* be together. It makes sense. There were years where we were not able to spend but a few hours together a couple days a week. I would tell friends "no" if plans would conflict with time for the two of us together. Something that started off as intentional and had a positive reward led to an automatic set of feeling laden with a sense of guilt and obligation. This is how operant conditioning can turn up in the relationship.

The brain becomes conditioned to have control or to react in certain ways when there is the potential for chaos or lack of control.

I hear from a lot of law enforcement couples about the eggshells in their relationship. I don't think law enforcement couples are unique in this, but we may be unique in how they get created in our relationship. They are created through operant conditioning.

To demonstrate this, I am going to create a story of John and Mary. We will pick it apart to look at the operant conditioning and how to remove these from your relationship. You might want to remember this story because it is one that I will probably return to over and over in order to share other skills to help your relationship. This story is based upon many that I hear about in my office and online.

John and Mary are in my office and telling me they are struggling. John is an officer of eight years and has been married to Mary for seven. They have two small children, ages three and five, and a retriever, Maggie, who they consider their first born. They have a good relationship. They know that they love one another and there is trust between them.

Mary shared that what she hates most is how she and the kids feel like they are on eggshells when John is home. She shares that the mood of the house changes and it feels like everyone is on high alert. The kids fight more and even Maggie acts up more when John is home. She says everything runs fine until John gets in the mix.

John says he feels like an outsider in his own home. There are days when the kids greet him at the door and he likes it, and other days when he comes home and they are yelling about something. His annoyance is that Mary doesn't understand that work is tough, and what he needs is the kids to be not fighting and calmer when he arrives home. He just needs some time to decompress and thinks that Mary doesn't want to understand what he needs.

Mary explains she does her best but that kids are kids and sometimes they are going to be upset. She goes on to also share that she doesn't appreciate the way John responds and yells at her and the kids, getting upset over the dumbest stuff. For example, Mary shares, "Kids spill milk, but John reacts as if it's some *huge* crisis. They drink out of plastic cups. Get a paper towel and clean it up. Instead he shouts and yells at the kids telling them to pay attention. The whole meal falls apart and no one wants to be at the table any more."

Mary continues, "We used to have fun when we were able to sit down to dinner together. Now I just wait for how it is going to end in disaster. " John retorts with, "She keeps telling me I have an anger problem. I don't know what the big deal is. I feel like an outsider and it bothers me when she says everything runs fine when I'm not home. When I am home, it's like I can't do anything right. I'm tired of her complaining and yelling at me for things. I think about going somewhere I'm more appreciated. I just don't think it's as bad as she is making it out to be."

As you read the story about John and Mary, you may be able to relate to it in some way. Some people, including mental health professionals, might read the story and assess that John has an anger problem. The assumption might then be that John needs to manage his stress differently with his family, which would then cause them to connect more. There might even be some thought about Mary and her parenting with the kids or her part in communication. If you consider the information that I gave you about conditioning, you may be able to see a different view.

When we consider conditioning and other factors that I talked about in the previous chapter, you might consider:

- John is coming down from hypervigilance when he arrives home. He may be edgy and/or tired.
- John's brain may set off his fight or flight response when the kids are loud or when the milk glass spills. (conditioning)
- John's brain has been conditioned to react in fight or flight situations. Fight or flight goes off and he needs to be "on" to fix the problem or the issues. (conditioning)
- Mary's brain has learned to potentially avoid the negative stimulus by keeping the kids quiet or calm. (conditioning)
- Mary's brain has also learned to avoid the negative stimulus and does not talk to John with respect or as a team. (conditioning)
- The kids are learning to avoid the negative stimulus, in this case John, as well as potentially learning to avoid him. (conditioning)

As a couple, we have to be careful to look at what may be underneath the problem, instead of just the problem itself. Having John work on his anger may be helpful, as it might help him control his reaction. What would be more helpful is for John to understand that amygdala of his is hijacking him and is starting to ruin the relationships he really wants to have in his life.

Mary could learn communication skills or boundary setting. It would be helpful for her to understand that her brain is seeing John as a potential threat (his big reactions and the vibe in the house), and trying to protect herself by shutting her down or sometimes yelling at him when he gets big. Both officers and spouses are impacted by this pattern of behavior. I have found that female officers handle conditioning a little differently due to the roles they must play. They experience conditioning just the same.

When experiencing eggshells, unless there is abuse, I believe both individuals are responsible. It is a natural response based upon operant conditioning for your brain to teach you to avoid a negative behavior or do a behavior to create a positive response. I am guilty of this in my own relationship. I did things out of kindness, but looking back I probably did some of those things to avoid my husband's frustrations when he came home.

Going back to the kitchen example, I would run my hand over the counter to ensure there were no crumbs. I even developed a technique for making sure there were no streaks on the stove top. It was ridiculous. Doing my best should have been enough. However, my husband's reactions caused my brain to go into overdrive to figure out how to avoid them rather than having a conversation to understand, *for five years*!

Yes, he could have told me that his reaction had nothing to do with me or just changed his reaction. I also had the responsibility to let him know how it was impacting me. We didn't know what we didn't know. In the solutions section, I will talk to you about the importance of honest vulnerable communication, boundaries, and owning behavior.

CONDITIONING IN COMMUNICATION

We have an open concept house and on the other side of our kitchen sink is a high counter. People stand there a lot when another person is in the kitchen cooking. I remember standing there one day while my husband was doing something in the kitchen and telling him a story about some interaction I had. I'm talking and telling my story when he looks up at me and makes a circular motion with his hand that indicates I need to hurry up. I stopped and looked at him, and he said something like, "get to the point." I remember staring and having a reaction of hurt and the thought of "F*** off you A**H***." Instead, I just said, "nevermind" and walked away. I felt totally dismissed and I was not going to say anything nice. He tried to tell me he wanted to know my point. I remember telling him that it wasn't about the point that it was about me sharing my life with him because we didn't see each other. I remember probably being emotional, angry, hurt, and dismissed at the same time. I didn't get to share with him because we were not together, and I couldn't share with him because he wanted the shortened factual condensed version. The phrase, "just the facts ma'am" from Dragnet reruns certainly applied in my relationship, and I found out that I wasn't alone in it.

Then, there is the *way* that I would be spoken to at times. There was a staccato directive voice that would emerge from time to time when we were driving or doing some chore that I had done literally thousands of times in my life. That tone in the voice can be authoritative and condescending. As a spouse, it is definitely a moment of "I'm not your citizen." It causes fights among couples mostly because many times that officer is totally unaware of how he sounds. His brain is conditioned to respond in a way in certain situations, and sometimes those are through verbal commands.

I remember bringing up this topic during an interview on the What's Your Emergency podcast, which is hosted by Justin, a firefighter/paramedic, and Jason, or MC, who is a motor jock cop (he takes pride in that). When I mentioned the way that cops can tend to communicate in stress and gave the example, he started chuckling. When I asked him about it, he said that he had done exactly that over the weekend with his wife. He shared that his kids were acting up. He had pulled the car over, pointed at her and said,

"You. Outside. Now." You can listen to the episode at http://wyeradio.com/episode37.

Before my husband and I had a conversation about it, I had just stopped talking to him. Seriously. There was a great deal of time that I told him just the facts of my day. He didn't know when I was struggling, sad, anxious, or what to celebrate with me. I cut him out. He really had no idea. It wasn't until I started talking again and sharing that he realized all I held back on. It hurt our relationship. I was in the relationship. I was faithful. I wasn't *in* the relationship. He wasn't a part of my world and he didn't really know or understand that he wasn't. I knew he picked up on it when he would say, "I just feel like we are drifting apart."

I tell my couples that they need to work to have a WAZE system for their relationship, constantly updated with "pothole on road ahead" or other such information in order to navigate communication and interactions. When you don't share, your love maps are not updated.

Dr. John Gottman has done over 40 years of research on couples. He classified them into two categories, the master's of relationships and the disasters of relationships. He and his wife, Dr. Julie Gottman, utilized the research to help couples and clinicians learn what is vital to keep a relationship intimate and thriving. One of the foundational pieces is [2]Love Maps, which are defined as knowing your partner's world.

When you are dating you start to learn about each other; your beliefs, family, hurts, accomplishments, dreams, desires, etc. This starts the map. The more you learn about each other, the more details get filled in. That map helps you to understand your partner's motivations, emotions, decision making, reactions, etc. I tell my couples that they need to work to have a WAZE system for their relationship, constantly updated with "pothole on road ahead" or other such information in order to navigate communication and interactions. When you don't share, your love maps are not updated. You can rely on old maps, but you may not get to your destination as quickly or you may wind up on a road with a lot of construction resulting in damage. The result from my husband's conditioned method of communication was a Love Map that was old and fading.

My husband was the one that helped me understand the communication SNAFU we were having between us. I wanted to take him on a journey of a moment in my life. He was listening for, or conditioned to listen for, what he needed to solve or fix. He told me about how he listens to complaints all day about one thing or the next. "People want to tell you the whole story about the situation and give you history that doesn't matter. Sometimes they want to tell me about bullshit that happened from five years ago. I'm wanting the facts to determine what I need to take care of the situation and if I need to enforce a regulation or law. I'm listening and deciding if this is a legal situation or just a bunch of people bitching about each other. Sometimes I get done on a scene and think, 'Well, that's an hour I could have spent doing something productive.'" He told me it's not that he didn't care about what I was saying, but that he had to be in the mind frame to sit and listen. I needed to let him know that I had a story to tell him so he could tell his brain it was ok to listen to the story. Ok. No, he didn't say it exactly like that, but that's what I'm telling you. Officers are also conditioned to respond in a certain way with their voices and their presence. You can see this come out during conversations as well. As a spouse, your brain interprets it as hostility and reacts accordingly.

One of the ways that spouses and families lose in the hypervigilance cycle is that it can make communication difficult. I already mentioned that in the recovery period of the cycle the prefrontal cortex is tired. It is in recovery mode. Because of that, spouses often receive minimal responses to conversation. Unfortunately, the HPA axis is ***not***! That pesky HPA axis is fully aware and without the prefrontal cortex to assist in interpreting the situation, the HPA axis rules the show. Here's how that plays out. A spouse is upset about something and has an elevated voice. The officer brain, on the downside of hypervigilance, hears the elevated voice and interprets this as danger. Because the prefrontal cortex is off-line, the HPA axis says, "This is stressful. We need to confront this in a big way and shut it down by getting big ourselves which may lead to something larger so let's gear up!" The result is an officer speaking loudly, yelling, and maybe being aggressive. If the prefrontal cortex would have been online, it would have told the HPA axis, "Hey! This is not a big deal. Calm down. This is not a real threat. This is someone safe. Stand down." Conversations become elevated when HPA is online and the prefrontal cortex is offline.

Another problem with conditioned communication is that officers are primed to resolve a situation. People communicate with them about problems that need to be solved. That is their purpose of listening to what the other person is saying. The brain becomes conditioned to look for the facts and the solutions to solve the problem. When there is communication about feelings, many times people just want to help and fix it. I don't think this is exclusive to law enforcement. As humans we want to help people, so we often want to fix rather than listen. Listening to feelings is a little different for officers. First, feelings are uncomfortable for officers as their brain usually helps them to avoid their own feelings to keep them safe. Many times when we talk about feelings, we are wanting to have someone respond with compassion and understanding in order to not feel alone. If you are talking to your officer spouse you may get something like, "well, that's bullshit" in return instead of that compassionate response. I talked about this in the previous chapter. It's that conditioned rejection. What is uncomfortable is bullshit and the person causing it is an asshole. It makes for an interesting conversation at times.

Knowing that there is conditioned communication in officers can help couples to knock down walls, like I had to do, and open up opportunities to have a different process for communication. I recommend the following process to my couples:

1. Let your spouse know you need to set up a time to chat.
2. Communicate the topic of the conversation including the reason for the conversation, and the potential result. (Just the facts, ma'am.)
3. Communicate the urgency of the conversation and deadline if there is one.
4. Share if this is a problem solving or a story sharing conversation.
5. Set up a time within the next week that works for both of you to have the conversation.

Implemented it looks like this:

1. I need to set up a time to talk to you for about 30 minutes.
2. I have a work situation going on. I want to share the details of what is going on and hope to get some emotional support and feedback on how I might handle the situation.
3. It's not super critical but sometime in the next 10 days would be great.
4. I just want to share the story. It's nothing you need to fix.
5. I know we both have some time Wednesday night. Would 5:30 work for you?

When you do this, don't forget to set a date and a time. Put it on the calendar. Make note of what you want to talk about so you don't lose what was going on at the time you wanted to chat.

WORKING AS A TEAM

Spillover is important to understand for both officers and spouses. Both must be diligent and pay attention to the potential of it impacting the relationship.

It is important to note that some behavior is not acceptable regardless if it is a reaction. These include behaviors that could be physically or emotionally intimidating and/or abusive, such as hitting, physical attacks, throwing objects, and attacks on someone's character.

While reaction may be a conditioned response for officers, they are also responsible for owning the behavior. Officers and spouses can work together to make changes in their relationship and minimize the impact of spillover.

1. **Establish a Ritual**: Officers need to establish a practice or [3]ritual on their way home that will allow them to re-enter their home life.
2. **Temperature check:** Text your spouse to let them know where you are mentally. You can do this on a scale of 1-10. 10 could be you are running hot and 0 could mean you are cool as a cucumber. Make the scale your own. It is loving and kind to let your spouse know where you are. If every day is a 10, other adjustments might need to be made. As a couple, you can talk about what this scale means and actions to take; for example, if 10 is sent, does that mean lots of hugs or some quiet time?
3. **Breathe Deeply**: Deep breathing is your body's way of knowing that things have calmed down. It will turn off the fight or flight response in your body and start the recovery process. Your body will start to stand down, which will help you when you get home.
4. **Intention:** What kind of person do you want to be when your spouse or family sees you after work? Setting the

intention in your mind will help you be that person when you walk through the door. Consider having a visual cue or trigger in the vehicle such a picture, love note, or drawing. This will help your brain change and get conditioned to wind down.

5. **Mood:** If you can, do something to shift the mood. Music and podcasts are a great way to do this. Stay away from the news. Quiet is always a great way to shift as well.
6. **Awareness**: Become aware of reactions and conditioning as a couple. Where there are blind spots, kindly help each other see them. Set up a time for conversation using the process above. Utilize ways to have difficult conversations talked about in Chapter (**). Awareness is key to change.
7. **Ownership**: Take ownership of your own behavior. This goes for officers and spouses. Stay out of defending it with phrases like, "I can't help it." Stay out of blame with phrases like, "Well, if X wouldn't have happened, I wouldn't have done Y!" Take ownership with phrases like, "You're right. That happened." Sometimes the ownership is the unwillingness to confront or have a difficult conversation.
8. **Seek Forgiveness**: Apologies are great, but just saying, "I'm sorry" is overused. Use "I apologize" instead of "I'm sorry." Seek forgiveness or apologize by first owning the behavior and asking your partner for forgiveness. Example, "I need to apologize to you. I overreacted to the milk. I get it. Will you forgive me? I'm going to work on it." Sometimes forgiveness is not easy. When a behavior happens over and over, there may be times your partner will not be ready to forgive you, but they may accept your apology.
9. **Allow Do Overs**: Fighting reactions and changing your brain will be tough. As a team, allow for failure and "do overs." Talk about setting up a phrase or a motion that will indicate a do over may be needed. The "time out" motion

works well for many couples. My husband will tell you that I am notorious for raising my left eyebrow up. When he sees this, he stops and says, "Let me try that again." Talk it over and find something that works for you that doesn't breed contempt or resentment.

Following the steps above will start to make change in the relationship and help you overcome the impact of conditioning.

THE CONFLICT

"You're working late *again*!" I was annoyed. It seems like he was the only one helping to pick up the shifts since they were short-staffed. "You are always there, and you never think about me!" Well, at least that is what I said in my head. What came out was probably worse, feigned indifference. "Whatever."

For the rest of the call, I was short and clipped, which caused my husband to call me out. "Why do you have to be like this! What do you expect me to do? I can't just say no!" My response? "Whatever." The call ended quickly after that. We saw each other sleeping. Talked little to each other, if at all, and eventually, it died down.

Effective communication and conflict are essential in relationships. I'll bet you a crap ton of money it's not what you are really needing.

Most of the couples in therapy or inquiries I get through my website and social media have one common element, "we need to communicate better." Effective communication and conflict are essential in relationships. I'll bet you a crap ton of money it's not what you are really needing. You may argue about the dishwasher being emptied or the trash being taken out or the time spent scrolling on the phone.

The majority of the time the argument, conflict, or communication is not about the topic of discussion. What is underneath is the need for connection. Couples want connection. As a law enforcement couple, we need connection. We have physical elements that make it difficult like shifts, sleep, and hypervigilance, and hidden psychological elements like conditioning, culture, and trauma.

I look back now at the arguments that we had like the one above. It is so apparent ***now*** that we both needed to feel heard and understood. He needed me to understand that he was making the choice not in spite of me but because he felt a duty to the guys that were going to be short and potentially at risk. I wanted to spend time with him. I felt like they got picked over me. If we had been able to communicate that, it would not have changed the situation, but it would have changed our support for each other.

One of my frustrations and my motivation to start Code4Couples® and write this book was that I could not find anything to help me understand what was going on in my relationship and what I needed to do about it. It was that moment of my husband reading *On Combat* by Lt. Col. Dave Grossman and us talking about mindset that helped me to have the initial "ah-ha" moment of there being something more than just the surface aspects I was reading and saw. I first learned what I needed to know and understand about the underpinning of how a career in law enforcement can impact the officer and the spouse. I then had to look at what I knew about relationships and connection.

I already mentioned Drs. John and Julie Gottman in the previous chapter. In case you skipped around, let me introduce them again. Dr. John Gottman has done 40 years of research on what makes couples work. His research determined what made couples succeed or fail. He asked and [1]recruited couples to come to his "Love Lab" in Seattle, WA. Couples would stay for several days at an apartment, as well as come to the research facility. Their interactions in the apartment were videotaped and then analyzed. Their vitals were taken regularly and their blood was drawn to determine if cortisol or other chemicals were being released into the bloodstream.

Dr. Gottman and his team would have the couple fight and also have them talk about their love story. He took all this information and categorized it to determine key elements necessary for a successful relationship. He also found elements that caused relationships to fail as well as identifying behaviors of 2 types of emotional abusers. The research is fascinating and is why I choose to utilize it with couples. His wife, Dr. Julie Gottman, is credited for getting the information out of the research journals and into the hands of clinicians and thus, couples. If you want to know more, I recommend you read *Seven Principles of Making Marriage Work* or go to one of the workshops. Another newer book is *Eight Great Dates.*

Knowledge is power, though, and I think it is important to examine how the relationship house can be damaged.

The Gottman's [2]Sound Relationship House is pivotal in understanding the struggles that come with a relationship and law enforcement. As I understood more and more about the world of law enforcement, my husband's world, and looked at the elements of a strong and fulfilling relationship, I could see more and more spillover. Don't worry. There are also solutions to all of this. Knowledge is power, though, and I think it is important to examine *how* the relationship house can be damaged.

After you know the how, you can then assess and repair. You can think of it like a real house. Maybe you are aware that there are cracks in the wall, but maybe you don't see the termites that are in the walls eating away the support beams. A home inspector is trained to look for problem areas and then tell you what you need to do to repair them. This information is going to allow you to be your own home inspector.

THE SOUND RELATIONSHIP HOUSE

There are nine components to a healthy relationship, which the Gottmans' have put in the [3]model of the Sound Relationship House. Damage to one part of the House has the potential to impact other aspects of the House. Using what you read in the previous chapters, you will read the definition of each element of the House as well as the potential conflict or impact from law enforcement. These aren't the only way the element can be impacted; it is what I see as the spillover from law enforcement. You can check out the house at www.holdthelinebook.com

TRUST

This is built on the belief that each partner acts and thinks to maximize the benefit to each other and not in self-interest. In law enforcement lingo, it's the belief that your partner has your "six." This belief is that before there is an action that is taken, there will be a filter of, "What would my partner think about this? How would they see this action? Does it honor them?"

Trust is not just about fidelity or infidelity. There are two other types of trust that I see couples struggle with.

- Emotional trust is sharing emotions and feelings, and trusting your spouse with those feelings. Will they honor the feelings or think they are ridiculous? It can also be about sharing information about your spouse with someone else instead of talking to them about it. I have had couples feel emotionally betrayed due to reading a text message to a friend that their spouse was being a "bitch" or "an asshole."

- Financial trust is another aspect of trust. Finances and money conversations are often difficult for couples and a source that can lead to financial betrayal. Financial trust involves disclosing debt, credit scores, and expenditures to each other. Financial betrayal occurs when a spouse finds out these elements later. This could mean taking out credit or a credit card and not informing your spouse. I have had couples that come in talking about not getting along only to find out that one of them is hiding $20,000 in credit card debt from the other one. Finance conversations are tough and the betrayal is painful.

Potential Impact

- Officers deal with people that lie all day long. Someone is pulled over for potentially driving while intoxicated but they "only had two". There are ten people standing when a crime happens but, "I didn't see anything." Officers deal with people trying to hide behavior all day. What I have learned along the way is that officers don't ask questions unless they know the answer, or should I say assume they know the answer. (This is important for later on in the chapter.) Their brain learns not to trust what people are saying. It's the saying, "If their mouth is moving, they are lying." I'm not immune to this. I work with people that cheat on their spouses and hear how they hide behavior. When I found out that my husband deletes all his text messages, my brain automatically jumped to the assumption he was hiding something. It's difficult to balance what you experience daily with the reality of your relationship. By the way, he deletes them because his phone can be taken for public record at any time.

- The conditioned response of reaction and fixing problems could lead to a struggle with emotional trust. I shared my story of my husband wanting me to get to the point. This felt like a hit to our emotional trust and I chose to not share as much emotional information. This could lead to loneliness and isolation and cause one or both spouses to seek emotional comfort elsewhere.
- When coming down from hyper-vigilance, the officer may not have the capacity to listen to their spouse, causing the spouse to not feel heard. The officer might commit to a chore or task in this state, not remember, and then fail to follow through.
- The officer's brain is used to getting hits of dopamine on a regular basis and can interpret daily or non-police life as boring. The brain finds ways to obtain the dopamine, which could be anything from having a really active to do list and not sitting still to spending money or having affairs, emotional or physical.

COMMITMENT

Commitment to one's partner means loving their attributes and growing in appreciation for those things that might otherwise be an irritation.

Commitment to one's partner means loving their attributes and growing in appreciation for those things that might otherwise be an irritation. This is also acting and believing that both partners are in the relationship for the long haul.

Maybe it's me but loving or appreciating attributes that drive you bananas is tough! I recommend looking at it as parts. Loving or appreciating that part because it is a part of your partner. Think of it as eating your brussel sprouts (ick) with the fabulous other food items on your plate. You take the whole plate.

Potential Impact

This is an area of the house that I fail to find an impact on. If anything, I think there is a positive impact as I see law enforcement couples committed to doing the hard stuff. Part of that might be knowing up front that law enforcement life is going to be hard.

Trust and Commitment are the walls of the house and when there are cracks in either of these, other elements in the house start to shift.

LOVE MAPS

Love Maps are the foundation of the House. The foundation for any relationship is friendship, along with knowing and understanding each other's worlds. If a map is not updated regularly, the user will not have the best understanding of how to get somewhere. If a Love Map is not updated, partners will not be able to truly know and understand each other.

> ***The foundation for any relationship is friendship, along with knowing and understanding each other's worlds.***

We have talked about this aspect of the House in the previous chapter. Couples need to continually learn about each other's lives, as many couples spend the majority of time away from each other at work or other activities. Interactions are important to share as they help partners and spouses to understand the players in a person's world. Couples need to keep up with the positive and negative interactions and events with the partner's world as well as the people in it. It is important to examine if you are not sharing a part of your Love Map with your spouse.

Potential Impact

- Shift work and recovery from hypervigilance can impact the couple's ability to connect meaningfully. Time passes without sharing stories and details are lost.
- Negative or painful calls or incidents may not want to be shared by the officer due to the brain wanting to avoid thinking about or recalling negative events or feelings.
- A spouse may have difficulty listening to the events or situation that their officer spouse encountered during the day and the negative emotional impact it has had and thus, not inquire or dismiss comments.
- Officers' brains are listening for facts and fixing rather than the journey and players in the story.
- Spouse is avoiding or predicting a reaction to a story or potentially feeling dismissed due to past interactions with the officer when they come home. Sometimes spouses will not share what happened with kids or a negative event due to reactions. I have not shared car trouble I have had with my husband for fear of a reaction.

FONDNESS AND ADMIRATION

Fondness and Admiration requires thinking fondly of and admiring one's partner, and believing they think and feel the same about you. In short, it is a culture of appreciation for each other in a relationship.

This layer of the house may sound woo-woo and sappy the way it is described. Think of it in terms of a "culture of appreciation." For this layer to be solid, you have to appreciate your partner and also feel appreciated by them. The appreciation can be verbal or non-verbal, but you better be clear about how your partner receives the appreciation. If you are buying gifts to show appreciation when all your partner wants is an "atta-boy," then you need to adjust and get clear. The popular book *5 Love Languages* is a good way to clear up appreciation. Appreciation can be expressed through acts of service, gifts, physical touch, words, or time. Couples need to be clear about how each other feels valued and appreciated.

Another aspect to this layer goes back to commitment and appreciating that quality in your partner that drives you bananas. My husband is a list maker. I am not. He puts it on the list and crosses it off. He will go until he is done and then rest. I kind of have a list, usually in my head, and it's almost always flexible. Confession.

Before I was married, there were times it was easier to just go get new underwear than do the laundry. I am that girl at the core. Early on, I was so impressed with my husband's ability to stay focused and get things done. He graduated from the academy when we were dating, and I figured he would procrastinate on finding a job. Nope. He made his list every day and did the thing. As we went along in our marriage, the list really started bothering me. I thought, "*Dude*, you are just adding crap to your list rather than playing with me!" I told him he needed to listen to the Toby Keith song "My List" and start living a little.

Another aspect to this layer goes back to commitment and appreciating that quality in your partner that drives you bananas.

I know my lack of organization drives him crazy, too. It's a simple thing that we do very differently. At some point in time, I realized I needed to stop fighting the list and embrace it. I spun the belief in my mind and appreciate that he has the desire to help around the house and get things done. I admire that he is known as the guy at work for "getting things done."

I'm not exactly sure how or if he appreciates my free-spirit mindset. Over the years, I have tried to become more list-oriented. It still doesn't work for me. I think it's the "hippie child" part of me. He tries a little more to be flexible. It's gotten to the point where I have asked him to coach me on how to "get things done." I'm a work in progress.

Potential Impact

- Officer brains are focused on the negative due to looking for infractions and interactions with people; thus, the negative is filtered in rather than the positive. The brain is looking for danger and not seeking out the positive and gratitude.
- Spillover from the officer seeing things negatively can cause the spouse and family to filter in negative.

TURNING TOWARD

Partners/Spouses "turn toward" each other daily in small ways such as sharing a joke, starting a conversation, or responding to emotional needs and support. When we interact with our spouse, we have the option to turn toward (stepping into their world), turn away (side-stepping their world), or turn against (fighting their world). Turning toward is walking into the spouse's world in order to see things through their perspective.

On the surface, people hear the concept of turning toward and think it's not so bad. John Gottman says to think of it as a [4]sliding door. You have to slide the door of the other person open and step in. Sometimes it's easy because there is something to celebrate, you want to back your spouse up, or support them in some way. It is difficult when you are in conflict, your spouse is struggling emotionally, or you don't agree with your spouse. Grief is a great example. When someone is grieving or lost someone they love, people show up initially. People give hugs, support, and casseroles. This is turning toward. Then things die down. People that were supportive avoid bringing it up or inviting you to events because it's uncomfortable. This is turning away. After months of grieving and sharing that you are struggling with the loss, people start telling you to get over it. This is turning against.

Gottman says we need to turn toward our partner over and over again. This is not easy when your spouse comes in the door irritated or pissed off, or you come home and your spouse unloads on you. Our first reaction is going to be our brain trying to keep us safe in a fight or flight response. If I come home and start yelling about the house, my husband does not say, "Wow honey. You seem really upset. Do you want to talk?" However, this is what Gottman is saying to do. Ugh, *right*!? When you see your spouse sitting on the couch staring mindlessly, it is sometimes easier to think, "I don't want to deal with that right now," and walk away. It's hard to turn toward and say, "I see you just staring. Are you struggling?"

Recently, my husband was struggling at work and I *felt* it. His demeanor was very "prickly." I could *feel* it. After probably a week, I said, "Hey, I don't know what's going on but I know it's something. I can feel it and it's impacting me, too. I'm here for you when you are ready to talk." Go ahead and call me out for turning away for a week. You're absolutely right. I did. I didn't want to say, "Do you want to talk?" only to be shut down. I needed to express to him that whatever he was dealing with was heavy, but he was being an asshole without me telling him he was being an asshole. So, I turned away. Once I got it out, I just kept telling him, "Hey, I know it's still on your mind so, whenever you are ready, I am." It was probably three weeks later when we were out for a really nice dinner at our favorite restaurant in downtown Dallas before he spilled. I remember thinking, "***Now***!? You pick *now* to talk!?" I was actually grateful that he decided to turn toward me and lean on me about his pain. I was sad that it took him so long, but sometimes it happens that way.

We have to turn toward our partner and trust that our partner is going to turn toward us. We are responsible for turning toward when we are struggling. It was hard to sit and trust that my husband was going to turn toward me. It was also not going to help our relationship if he wasn't willing to turn toward me with what was impacting him. It has to be reciprocal. We have to lean on each other and walk toward the person, even if it is uncomfortable. That is how intimacy is built. Deep dive on this coming later in the chapter!

Potential Impact

- Blue family culture has a mentality of "be strong," which is misinterpreted as "sucking it up."
- Culture can dictate that needing to lean on someone is a weakness, so I will not choose to turn toward or will look at someone who "needs" as weak.
- Officer wants or needs to be seen as the hero.
- Reactive responses prevent officers or spouses from turning toward.
- Spouses struggle to hear the hard stuff and don't listen, or the spouse does not share.
- Officers often want to protect their family from what they see or experience and so there is a lack of sharing of the difficult stuff.
- The brain wants to repress or avoid negative emotions, which could cause turning away.

POSITIVE PERSPECTIVE

The positive perspective is the ability to offer a positive or generous explanation for events. This perspective can cushion or soften difficult conversations and prevent conflicts from spiraling out of control.

The positive perspective helps us to provide a situation or person the benefit of the doubt. Applying the positive perspective allows us to generously interpret a behavior, conversation, or action in a positive manner. If someone cuts me off in traffic and I provide a positive perspective, I may think the person simply didn't see me, and sometimes I have done the same thing. My reaction is then minimized because my brain does not see the interaction as a threat. If your spouse sighs in the middle of a conversation, the positive perspective would be that they needed to take a breath, or they are starting to relax.

If you can keep a positive perspective, it can protect the friendship layer on the house as well as help you to have healthier conflict.

The opposite of the positive perspective is negative sentiment override. I think of it as slime in your relationship. Or since we are talking about your house, it would be the termites, eating away at the wood holding your house together. Each level of the house can insulate or impact another layer. If you can keep a positive perspective, it can protect the friendship layer on the house as well as help you to have healthier conflict. If your spouse sighs in the middle of a conversation and you have negative sentiment override, the sigh is interpreted as boredom or disinterest.

The perspective has a great impact on the story that we create around an event. Remember, our brain is wired for survival. It is wired to keep us safe and not make us happy. Our brain is naturally going to think the negative first. We must work against it and provide a possible positive explanation. There are some great tricks I have for this, which I will share in the next chapter. I will share that nine times out of ten, what is happening is not about you. I had to learn this. Consider my kitchen situation. I thought for years, it was about me. Couples get upset about situations and take it personally. Sometimes the positive perspective can be, "We love each other. We can work things out even when it's difficult."

Potential Impact

- Officers are conditioned to have a negative perspective. If they see a situation, they must assume and prepare for the worst. This goes for every interaction they have as they know the simplest traffic stop could lead to injury or death.
- Spouses are impacted because they learn the dark side. Knowing that people's intentions are not always good, reinforces the brain to scan for other negative reasons for people's interactions.

MANAGING CONFLICT

Managing conflict focuses on being able to solve problems or move "gridlocked" issues to a problem that can be solved. It involves knowing how to start a conversation, accepting influence, repairing, de-escalating, and the ability to compromise.

The conflict layer of the house is one layer of the house, but *man* is it a *layer*! There are multiple components within the term conflict, and each one of those is a potential skill that a couple can learn. Many people assume that conflict is negative. Conflict can be positive. It can lead toward resolution or growth. If a couple can assume a positive perspective toward conflict, couples can learn to look forward to difficult conversation and an opportunity to learn about each other, and then come to a resolution that honors them both.

That is *not* how most couples see conflict, nor how I saw conflict for a long time. We learn to have conflict based upon how it was handled in our family. It runs the spectrum of unhealthy families yelling and throwing things, to families that don't have conflict at all. Whatever your experience, the way you handle conflict has a foundation of how you experienced it as a child. While conflict was not a negative experience for me growing up, we rarely had conflict. When I experience conflict, my brain automatically jumps to fight or flight and I try to shut it down. This means I also try not to have it. I really had to work on this as it is my *job* to confront people about behavior or toxic thought patterns. I had to learn how to have conflict. Other people have to unlearn unhealthy conflict skills.

It's important to remember that conflict, any conflict, is probably going to elicit a fight or flight response. It's wired in. Success depends on your conflict skills, but other elements are important.

- Understand personal experiences with conflict. Learning the family experience and past relationship experience is important. Raised voices, manipulation, violence, passive-aggressive behavior, control, or lack of conflict impact the way our brain interprets conflict.
- Triggers. Understanding what triggers the fight or flight response in yourself and your spouse can help to ensure successful conflict. Saying, "calm down" in the middle of an argument may be about your struggle with loud voices. It may trigger your partner feeling dismissed or silenced. Maybe a previous partner used tears to manipulate, which would cause a possible reaction to tears.

- Positive Perspective. Staying in the positive mindset such as "we can solve this" can help a couple to be more successful.
- No Matter What. It's important to have "no matter what" thoughts to calm your fight or flight response. These can be phrases like, "no matter what we love each other" or "no matter what he/she is not leaving". Establish your "no matter what" statements with each other when you are not in conflict. Early in my relationship, I established a "no matter what, he loves you" statement for myself because my immediate reaction to conflict was that my husband would want to leave the relationship. I have also established a "no matter what my thought and opinion matter... say it with kindness" statement because I tended not to speak up for myself.
- Turning Toward. It is in conflict that we *must* turn toward each other. You have to get curious about the other person's thoughts. If you don't do this, you will stay in an attack-defend mode and go nowhere. It's tough. Do it anyway.

We could go through each element of the house and talk about how they impact conflict. Just like officers go to the range, run drills, practice defensive tactics, and go through active shooter scenarios in order to prepare for altercations, couples must practice the way they communicate and strengthen all aspects of their house to prepare for successful conflict.

Potential Impact

- Officers are conditioned to "win." If they "win" they come home at night and they keep control of the scene. This "win" mindset tends to make officers want to control rather than "volley". This impacts the fight or flight response and can make it difficult for an officer to shift mindset and listen to their spouse. When I work with officers and tell them they are trying to win, they say, "absolutely!"

- Conditioned to "win" (Part 2). As officers are conditioned to "win," compromise can become difficult. The mindset is if they are not winning, they are losing. This mindset can lead to an officer just agreeing rather than risking the loss if they choose to say something different.
- Officer's brains are conditioned to reject negative feelings and emotions as "bullshit" and the people causing the discomfort as "assholes." (Gilmartin) This also applies to conflict with the spouse and can result in discussions and conflicts being dismissed emotionally (stonewalling or shutting down) or physically (walking away).
- Authoritative Spillover. The authoritative tone that officers use to control a scene or a situation comes out in conflict. This can cause a spouse to feel dismissed or feel manipulated.
- React vs Respond. Officer's brains are conditioned to react and not respond. The officer's brain wants them to act upon the potential danger rather than responding. The fight or flight response is primed to act, which makes it difficult to listen and respond to the situation.

The upper part of the house includes two components which I have combined in the explanation as they overlap a bit.

MAKING LIFE DREAMS COME TRUE

Helping your partner realize their dreams and aspirations is a big part of relationships. This may include play, fun, adventure, and purpose.

CREATING SHARED MEANING

Creating a shared meaning involves the couple finding meaning and purpose, and might drive the way a couple utilizes their resources of time and money. This might involve the way you influence or impact your family, culture, beliefs, and/or the legacy you want to leave behind.

These two aspects of the house may overlap. As a dating couple you found things in common and some of those were probably activities, dreams, goals, values, beliefs, or maybe even a legacy you wanted to leave behind. Maybe you had a common dream of traveling, found that you both like hunting or other activities, had the same desire to raise a family, or any other number of dreams or meaning for life. Making life dreams come true is also supporting your partner in their dreams. If your spouse's dream is to be the best law enforcement officer they can be, what does that mean and how do you support it? It can be difficult to do when that dream or meaning includes sacrifice. Both partners need to be supportive with each other, but also look at boundaries or compromise.

If your spouse's dream is to be the best law enforcement officer they can be, what does that mean and how do you support it?

As a law enforcement officer who wants to impact your family and leave a legacy to your children, you may sacrifice time and sleep in order to make sure that you spend time with your children. As a law enforcement spouse, you may or may not have understood that with the officer's commitment comes a commitment from you as well. That is not something I understood when I encouraged my then fiancé to go for his dream of being a cop.

There can be conflict in the dreams and meaning, and I encourage couples to visit how their dreams and meaning have shifted. At one time, I was so burned out at the non-profit I worked for that I begged my husband to get behind me finding something else even if it meant a pay cut. He couldn't do it. I understood but was hurt because the message I got was his security and money was more important than my happiness and well-being. Two years later, I was leaving due to other circumstances, starting a private practice, and doing contract counseling work. We've talked about it since and he has said that he regrets not hearing how miserable I was and supporting me. His own fears got in the way, and potentially maybe even some past relationships stuff where he was taken advantage of.

Early on in our marriage, my father-in-law passed away. A scholarship was started at the high school he attended as a part of his will. The scholarship is based upon financial need and provides tuition for the private Catholic high school. As we became more financially stable and were unable to have children, my husband asked if we could make the financial sacrifice to add to the scholarship fund. It was important to him to impact the education of others that cannot afford it and that his father's legacy lives on. We have other dreams and shared meaning, such as the legacy and impact I hope to make with this book and dreams of staying for a month at a time away in a Tuscan hillside town drinking wine and making friends with wine makers.

I encourage the two of you to dream and brainstorm. Start a Pinterest board, hang pictures, meaningful quotes, or design a vision board for your life together. One of the challenges I give to couples is to jointly list 100 things they would like to do as a couple, big or small. It can be experiences, places, recipes to cook, or whatever you want. Anytime you feel like you are on the hamster wheel of life, go look at the list, add to it, or pick something to do. We just have a shared file in Evernote that holds ideas and articles that we have about our future. We bring up the conversation when we need to have some hope and recalibrate due to stress. It provides us stability and purpose.

Potential Impact

- Gilmartin states that one of the consequences of hypervigilance is "usta syndrome." I "oust" do this. I "usta" do that. It's an easy cycle to fall into with the lack of motivation or ability to make decisions during the recovery of hypervigilance. Make plans ahead of time to prevent falling into the cycle.
- The officer's constant interaction with the negative impacts the view of humanity, family, culture, beliefs, and faith. A couple may start off with similar views, which then change and become conflictual due to the officer's humanity and beliefs being impacted.

INTIMACY – WHAT DOESN'T WORK

It had been a slow slide. I had seen the change in my husband over the years. There were times when I felt dismissed and like he thought I was an idiot. He was always sure to tell me he loved me, but his actions and words weren't always congruent. Mine began to not be as well at times. I was probably more accommodating than I needed to be; besides, he had a tougher life than I did. Wasn't it my job to be supportive and learn to cope with it? At least that is what I had been trying to do up to that point.

But once again, the department was taking priority and I was tired of the spillover. We had been married for about twelve years and I was done feeling the feelings and trying to cope. I wasn't done with the relationship, but I was done feeling the impact of life. In my mind, I left and shut down. I learned to "turn off" long ago, and I was doing that to him. I was still there physically. I still loved him immensely.

We didn't really fight that much because I went with the flow. I was growing my own business and I dove into it. I didn't share because most of the time, he wasn't around that much. When he was, I would share briefly because I had been trained not to story-tell. I got to the point and said what I needed to say. I want to be clear that on the outside, and even to him, things appeared "fine." I was dutiful. We would still have fun, go hunting, cook together, enjoy wine, chit chat, and have sex. None of that changed. What had changed was our intimacy.

It is in intimacy that people feel deeply loved. Intimacy can be thought of as, "into me, you see."

In the previous chapter, I went through what my husband calls the "mechanics." So now that you have the mechanics, let me give you the romantic. I'm not talking romance like in a movie; I'm talking about the romance of intimacy. It is in intimacy that people feel deeply loved. Intimacy can be thought of as, "into me, you see." Intimacy is about feeling that you are deeply known and that you deeply know your partner.

If you are an officer, it's the difference in understanding your weapon and knowing your weapon. You can understand the mechanics and have knowledge of how it works. You can even practice and hit targets. You can take it apart and put it back together. You need to be able to feel the firearm, how it responds to you, listen to it to determine if something sounds off. You need to be intimate with the firearm.

There was a beautiful cartoon I saw recently that described this. Two figures sat on cliffs opposite from each other holding spoons with long handles. On a cliff in between them was a pot of honey. The figures dipped their spoons into the honey trying to feed themselves but failed due to the spoon handle being so long. They could not reach their own mouth. The figures then realized that they needed to feed each other which then caused their isolating cliffs to come together on solid ground. The idea and the concept are poetic. We must feed each other in a relationship. Great in theory. There are elements that get in the way in all relationships, and there are unique elements in law enforcement relationships that impact our intimacy.

Dr. Sue Johnson talks about intimacy in relationships and the concept of emotional vulnerability. She speaks of the necessity of emotional vulnerability within a relationship in order to have intimacy in her book *Hold Me Tight* (which I recommend). Dr. Johnson discusses how intimacy is created at the beginning of our relationships, much like Dr. Gottman discusses Love Maps. Dr. Johnson talks about how we take time to really know our partner, to truly see who they are and share ourselves with them. This creates the intimacy and closeness that we feel at the beginning of our relationships. We are attentive to our partners, and in that trust and attentiveness, we connect. As we go through our relationship, our attentiveness wanes and the attachment is threatened. She talks about how events and our hurts become incorporated into ways that we protect ourselves and also threaten attachment.

Lonely is our body's way of telling us to reach out and connect.

Our brain reacts to that threat and starts to put up barriers to prevent connection. That protection then impacts our ability and willingness to be vulnerable and connect. The barriers our brain has learned to create to keep us safe often get in the way of the risk and vulnerability that is necessary to maintain feeding each other. Left unaddressed, the attachment, connection, and intimacy may continue to decline, leaving us feeling lonely.

Lonely is our body's way of telling us to reach out and connect. If we are feeling a lack of attachment and connection, the bonds have to be repaired through reaching out, connection, and emotional vulnerability.

Let's rewind a little. I have brought up a point in time in my relationship that I had shut down. We weren't fighting in our relationship. Our sex life was good. My husband told me what a "hottie" I was. We told each other, "I love you." We liked to go out for nice meals and enjoyed sitting on the porch talking and catching up with elements of our day when we could. I was past the point of not knowing what to do with my time when he was gone. I had figured out the stuff that a lot of people talk about when being married to a law enforcement officer. On the outside, it looked like I was nailing the law enforcement life. I didn't share any differently. I wrote earlier, I was married but I wasn't *in* my marriage. I was going through the motions. I didn't know any different.

All the older couples pretty much told me, "You just have to deal with it. This job is going to change them and you have to adjust." I thought it was crap and that I had to suck it up. The job seemed more important than our relationship. I felt stuck. Say something about what I thought and look like an unsupportive bitch. Say nothing and struggle with growing resentment and shut down. I chose the shut down. I just didn't share. On the outside, it all looked good. I had mastered this skill as a teenager struggling with self-worth, anxiety, and depression. Crying and dying on the inside, yet looking well-adjusted and happy on the outside. My brain fell back on old patterns of behavior and neuropathways and the disconnection grew.

Sometime around 2011 or 2012, I was working with a client and they asked if I had seen Brené Brown's Ted X Talk on vulnerability. I had not. She showed me a little and I promised to go home and watch it so we could discuss it later. When I watched it at home, I was inspired and mortified at the same time.

If you have not heard of Dr. Brené Brown or her Ted talks, I recommend that you watch the [1]Ted X Talk "The Power of Vulnerability." The video has 2.2 million views the day I'm writing this. I was so impacted by the video and her research that I became a certified facilitator for her Daring Way™ program. (CDWF) There are many aspects of her research that impacted my life and who I have become. The relationship lesson I learned was: connection, depth, and intimacy in a relationship is created through vulnerability. Ick.

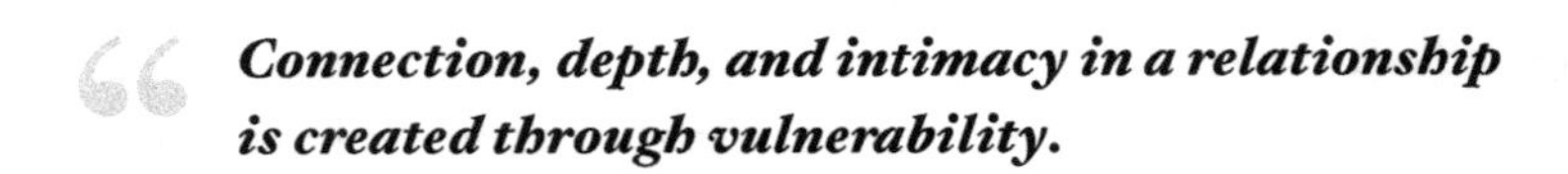

Connection, depth, and intimacy in a relationship is created through vulnerability.

As I dug into what it really meant to be connected, I noticed a word that kept coming up and I didn't exactly like it, *vulnerability*.

THE V WORD

I had an officer in my office. His wife had an affair with a coworker, and he was struggling. At one point in time, they saw me as a couple to heal their relationship. He had stormed out of my office during one session and never came back. Now, a year later he sat on my couch. I felt the emotional armor on him. It was like an invisible force field around him. I confronted him and told him he felt prickly like a cactus and whatever he was trying to keep covered up was not going to get better until he was willing to be open and vulnerable. He cracked and told me he was so mad at his wife one night that he hit her. She felt she deserved it. He felt shame because he saw himself as something he never wanted to be.

Vulnerability is something that our body rejects and tries to protect us from. Yet, it is one of the most crucial elements to making us feel connected.

We worked through it with him being open and vulnerable with me and then his wife. We talked about him building a "new" and better marriage. I talked about the feelings of vulnerability he would have to be willing to experience when extending trust and how to move through them rather than reacting or numbing which were his go-to responses.

After several sessions and things moving in a positive direction for him, we were again discussing uncomfortable feelings of vulnerability and he said something like, "I get it! It's the 'V-Word'!" He was my first client that started calling vulnerability "the V word" like I had just sworn at him. It just kind of stuck.

So, what the heck is vulnerability? Play along with me for 30 seconds.

Here is what I want you to do:

- Set a timer for 30 seconds.
- When I say, "Go", I want you to take a deep breath in and out.
- Pay attention to your body. Notice tension, your breathing, your heartbeat, and just sit for a couple of seconds.
- Then, think about or say "vulnerability" to yourself and pay attention to what your body does.
- Ready? *Go*
- Done? Good!

What did you notice? Did your stomach flip? Did you cringe a little? Did you notice your body rejecting the word? I'm going to guess that not one person reading this thought, "Oh yea! That sounds exciting!" I doubt that anyone's body relaxed or suddenly got excited in a positive way.

Vulnerability is something that our body rejects and tries to protect us from. Yet, it is one of the most crucial elements to making us feel connected.

Brené Brown defines [2]vulnerability as emotional risk or exposure. Yeah, that sounds great. Let's do *so* much more of that (said with great sarcasm). Based upon her research, vulnerability was a key element in people living congruent, authentic, and "wholehearted" lives. Vulnerability is about "being seen". Vulnerability is not airing your whole life story in front of a stranger. There is an authenticity that comes with vulnerability, a genuineness about content and emotion. It *feels* connecting. If you are the one sharing, it feels exposing.

Brief recap: emotional vulnerability is necessary to maintain intimacy and connection. Without it, we feel lonely. When the connection is threatened our brain starts to protect itself because it is there to keep us safe, not make us happy, which in turn makes us resist the *one* thing that can really help us feel connected, reaching out in emotional vulnerability.

Now, let's throw in some law enforcement related issues to make this even more challenging!

VULNERABILITY IS NOT WEAKNESS

On the job, I do *not* want officers to be vulnerable. I want them to have the equipment and tools to protect themselves so they can go home at night. I want them to have the psychological tools to be mentally and physically safe as well. This means taking off the emotional armor that protects them on the job. It can be a challenge for officers to understand that they need to learn how to put on and take off their emotional armor to be vulnerable with their spouse. It is also a challenge for spouses to take off their own emotional armor and be vulnerable with their officer. In a culture that values "strength", to think about becoming emotionally vulnerable seems to naturally imply weakness.

If an officer shares that they are struggling with another officer at work, there is a vulnerability that they will not be trusted the next time they have to go on a scene or conduct a building search. It is often the fear of how we are going to be seen by the other person that keeps us from sharing what we want, or ultimately need to share with the person we need to be closest to, our spouse. Spouses and officers often spend much of their relationship being "strong" for each other, thinking that this is supportive. As a spouse, I wanted to appear supportive and so I chose not to talk about how I was being impacted with my husband. I stuffed much of my worries and fears and didn't share. I didn't want to burden him. He was doing the same and didn't want to burden me. Getting past the idea that emotional vulnerability being a weakness may be difficult.

Law enforcement couples can relate to courage. Officers run toward the danger while others are running away. At some point in time, as a couple, you realize the courage it takes to show up call after call and scene after scene. As an officer, I hope you realize the courage it takes for your spouse to watch you walk out the door knowing that there is always the potential that you will be physically or psychologically injured today or over the years of service that you give to your community. Courage is an act. The act of courage involves vulnerability. No one ever did anything brave without being vulnerable. When you reframe the idea of vulnerability into courage, we can connect to it and it doesn't seem quite as "weak".

EMOTIONAL ARMOR

In order for emotional vulnerability to be effective, both partners have to be able to be open and willing to be vulnerable. If one partner shares but the other cannot receive it, the brain will learn that person is not safe, leading to further disconnection and loneliness. This can also lead to a partner turning toward someone who is safe which can lead to emotional and physical affairs. Both partners have to make sure to take off their emotional armor.

As I mentioned above, emotional armor is part of what keeps us being able to do what we do as a law enforcement couple. Our brain has to somehow push out the vulnerabilities to our partner, whether it is an officer going on the job or a spouse at home that you cannot protect. Emotional armor also protects the officer from being continually impacted by what they experience or see on the job. The brain has to figure out a way to cope. There are several techniques that the brain uses for emotional and psychological armor, all of which impact the couple's ability to connect through emotional vulnerability.

COMPARTMENTALIZING

I hear from many people when they experience trauma, grief, or negative feelings that they compartmentalize them. When I ask about thoughts or anxieties about the event, they tell me they just mentally put it in a box and put it on their shelf. When I ask about how the event or situation has continued to impact them, they tell me it hasn't. I laugh, in my head. I used to think the same thing, that the events that I had experienced in my life did not impact the way I thought about others or situations. These events were incidents that I could put away in a box and put on a shelf with the ability to ignore or just notice every now and then it was there. The fact is your brain is constantly collecting information and learning what it needs to be on high alert for. You may not *think* events have impacted you. They have!

If I haven't made the point clear already, the officer's brain becomes conditioned on how to cope with the events and one of those ways is to figuratively shove it in the corner of the brain. It happens and they move on. Spouses are not immune to this. The emotional armor that is used to protect on the job comes home to protect as well and impacts the connection.

Let me use an example to explain. A couple is out in the garage on a hot day working on a project needing to be done. In the stress of the project and heat, the officer gets upset at the situation and yells at their spouse. They take a break to cool off and nothing more is said. The spouse is waiting for the officer to take some ownership or connect after the situation, but nothing comes. The spouse may react but ultimately what has happened is there was an emotional injury and the officer failed to repair. The spouse's brain then learns, "You gotta be careful. That guy loses his temper and thinks he has the right to do so." The officer's brain on the other hand may have compartmentalized the situation. There was a blow up; there was a break; we moved on. It is a result of going call to call. There is no processing. Sometimes when a spouse tries to process or share how it hurts, they are met with something like, "get over it". The injury remains unless or until the couple is willing to experience some emotional vulnerability.

Spillover also occurs as a part of compartmentalizing.

All those boxes cannot stay on the shelf all of the time. Sometimes an emotion or event triggers them all falling off the shelf. If you have an image of someone having those boxes stacked so they are perfectly but precariously balanced, even one more box can set off all of them falling. Many times, those events happen at home since that is the place that the officer can take off their emotional armor. Unfortunately, we let emotions out where we feel safest and they do not always come out in a kind and caring way.

While compartmentalizing is effective on the job, it is not effective as a way of living. If we are going to be connected and intimate as a couple, we must be willing to share and appropriately dispose of or integrate events through sharing of emotions and thoughts and practicing gratitude.

SHAME

When we are asking ourselves or being asked to be emotionally vulnerable, the way we see ourselves or the way we fear being seen by others gets in the way of opening up to one another. I mentioned this earlier when I spoke about vulnerability as weakness. Dr. Brené Brown shares a way to have insight into your own [3]shame. Answer this sentence stem: "In my relationship, I do not want to be perceived as ______________, ________________, ________________." Many times I hear words like broken, weak, fragile, uncaring, not in love, and an asshole. The answer to this sentence stem is usually our own shame and why we resist opening up into emotional vulnerability with our spouses.

Shame is human and not unique to law enforcement culture. People tend to use the word guilt when they mean shame. Guilt is, "I do not like my behavior." Shame is, "I am a bad (or other negative word) person." Guilt can be a useful motivation to change. Shame is a demotivator and separates us from others. Let me use parenting as a way of demonstrating the difference between guilt and shame. Let's say a child lies about something. Guilt would be, "I'm disappointed you chose to lie. In this house, we respect the truth even though it means there may be consequences." Shame parenting would be, "You're a liar and liars are punished!" You might see it as a subtle difference. The brain sees it drastically differently. Shame initiates the fight or flight response and isolation. Guilt may feel bad but also leaves a person with the ability to change a behavior.

I have spoken to officers after an incident when they were injured, and they are sitting and rolling in feelings of shame due to the injury. On episode 54, Surviving an Officer Involved Incident as a Couple: Greg and Jaelyn Lovell, of my Code4Couples® Podcast, talked about the shame he felt in just saying the word "help" after he was overtaken in a situation. My husband was on a scene in full tactical gear in over 100 degree heat and as the situation was winding down, his officers started to notice he was not making sense and starting to be incoherent. He felt shame and I believe his words were, "like a weak bitch" for having to go to the hospital due to dehydration. Shame is a human emotion and left unaddressed, it leads to negative behaviors and emotional consequences. In a field where all negative emotions are avoided, shame is a killer, literally.

Being aware of shame in ourselves and in our spouses is a necessary and uncomfortable part of emotional vulnerability and taking off emotional armor. Watch for words like "should have" or phrases that seem to indicate that the person is "not good enough" or "not enough". Watch for withdrawn behavior or avoidance of topics in a conversation which can mean a redirecting of the conversation or a blow up when the topic is brought up. Getting curious about the behavior can be difficult but it can also allow you or your spouse to open up and share the struggle occurring.

EMOTIONAL ARMOR

In addition to compartmentalizing, Dr. Brown has found three other types of [4]emotional armor that we use as humans. These are Foreboding Joy, Perfection, and Numbing. When I lay these out, spouses, you may have an "ah-ha" moment like I did. Officers, you may just say, "well, shit!" Emotional armor is our brain's way of keeping us safe from what it sees as a threat, albeit an emotional threat, but a threat nonetheless.

While that emotional armor can be helpful in certain situations, it ultimately starts impacting our life. In therapy, I tell my clients that many times the problems they are having now are due to coping skills needed at one time but now no longer needed. Our armor can be the same way.

Perfection

When we are emotionally injured in some way, our brain tends to think, "If I am more perfect then the negative thing that happened to me won't happen again." It can also work in reverse, "If I don't do that thing (or try that thing), I won't fail and thus I will avoid the injury." Perfection is a way that our brain tries to avoid vulnerability. It's a "hustle" because the fact is that we will never be perfect for everyone or in every circumstance.

In law enforcement relationships, some of these elements are intensified. The officer who is conditioned to get things "right" or be on top so they can get control and go home at night, may struggle more with perfection or insist on perfection from the people they are with in order to avoid some implied danger which could include being seen negatively. Black and white thinking of legal vs. illegal leaves little room for the "grey" in life. This spills over to the family and children of officers. Children often feel they must be perfect in the eyes of the officer either because it is stated or implied.

Foreboding Joy

Sometimes our brain decides that it feels too vulnerable when becoming excited or happy due to the potential of being let down or the "other shoe dropping". It can also be that the brain has been so exposed to pain that it feels that it must protect due to the potential of bad things happening. This can also connect to Drs. Gottman's positive perspective. This could be as simple as not getting excited about a vacation because something might happen, and we don't want to jinx it. It can also be looking at your spouse and thinking how much you love them and how much they could break your heart in the same moment.

Officers spend an inordinate amount of time seeing the negative in humanity. Foreboding joy is another way of thinking of cynicism.

They are trained and conditioned to think through how something could go wrong. Their brain is *conditioned* to avoid or forebode joy and positive emotions.

Numbing

This occurs when the brain wants to block the negative feelings and uses something else to distract from the feelings. The brain could feel uncomfortable sitting in quiet. The brain can say, "uncomfortable!" and you pick up your phone and start scrolling. Numbing usually occurs as a lack of being mindful and present to our situation. Ironically, anything that can be used to comfort can be used to numb. We can use many things to comfort including food, sex, alcohol, chocolate (it's a different category than food in my eyes!), working out, reading, video games, helping others, and religion to name a few. Moderation is an important factor. The other difference between the two is the feeling after the behavior has occurred. We may enjoy streaming some of our favorite shows but after hours of watching we feel like a slug and I usually think of all the things I "should have been" doing during that time. That is when I know I have been numbing. Anything in moderation. If you aren't being mindful and using moderation, you are numbing.

Numbing usually occurs as a lack of being mindful and present to our situation.

In protecting the officer, the brain naturally numbs feelings. It tries to numb the darkness and negative that it experiences. Unfortunately, you cannot numb the dark without numbing the light. As the capacity for feeling negative feelings diminish, so does the capacity for positive. This could be considered numbing as well as foreboding joy. Due to the officer's lack of connecting with feelings within their body, an officer is at risk for numbing behavior. When feelings are involved, numbing the feeling is one of the first ways the brain is going to try to cope.

THE STRUGGLE WITH EMPATHY

A component necessary for emotional vulnerability, connection, and intimacy is empathy. Empathy is the ability to understand and share feelings. We connect *with* people through empathy. We experience empathy and feel heard and seen when someone expresses empathy. We feel that they understand us on a deep level. There is a difference between sympathy and empathy. Sympathy conveys, "it sucks to be you over there struggling like you are." It conveys pity and sorrow. Sympathy is feeling for someone. I *hate* sympathy cards. "Sorry for your loss" does not convey that you understand me. Sympathy sends a casserole. Empathy sits next to me while I cry knowing that there is nothing you can say to make it better. Empathy is hard. Empathy is a choice. Empathy connects us.

Teresa Wiseman has 4 elements of expressing [5]empathy:

1. Taking the perspective of the other person. This involves being able to take a moment to think what it would be like to be that other person.
2. Staying out of judgement. When expressing empathy, we have to be able to stay out of a negative perspective or judgement of the person's actions, behavior, or experience.
3. Recognizing emotions in others. Listen to the person's tone, words, and inflection and pay attention to their facial expressions so you can determine what emotion they are expressing or feeling.
4. Communicating the emotion. People get tripped up communicating emotion. Many times they want to make it more complicated. It's more about the way you are saying it, using your tone, inflection, and facial expression rather than what you are saying.

The hard part about empathy is that it involves finding a similar feeling within yourself. As humans, we do not have similar experiences. We *do* have similar feelings. When I am with couples in my office explaining the concept of empathy, I state feelings and have the couple raise their hand if they have felt the feeling in the past. We have felt joy, excitement, anticipation, fear, surprise, pain, grief, and sadness. The feelings might be different depths due to experiences, but we have felt them. For example, you might not know what it is like to lose one of your best friends. You may have experienced grief in the past and be able to remember the pain that comes from losing something.

Empathy is a skill. We are not born with empathy. It must be modeled for us or we must be taught to consider what it feels like to be the person in different situations. Empathy takes practice. It is common for the couples I work with to use too many words when they express empathy. They make it too complicated, trying to say it right, rather than focusing on feeling the feeling. It is always better to try to connect even if it means that you say, "that sounds so painful and makes me sad." Sometimes just saying, "ouch" with feeling to a person's pain, is empathy.

I sit with people in empathy all day. I feel with them and they feel understood. I haven't been through what many of them have been through or struggle with, yet they feel understood. *That* is the power of empathy.

You may have already picked up on some struggles with this concept based upon some of the things I have discussed already. The core of empathy is to tap into a feeling somewhere within your body. An officer's brain can potentially want to shut down the ability to access certain feelings due to the fear of unleashing some kind of avalanche of emotions that have been compartmentalized or repressed. It takes practice and courage for officers to tap into emotions for this very reason. They may be able to express their own emotions but struggle to connect with others. When someone expresses empathy, we can feel the connection. Many times, when officers try to express empathy, it may come out flat but they are trying to express that they understand and connect.

Judgement is a struggle for officers also due to the conditioning and the cynicism that we have discussed. I shared the story about my iPhone being stolen earlier in the book. My husband's judgement of my behavior would have prevented him from having empathy. He was unable to empathize with someone he saw as a "sheep." Judgement can get in the way for either partner. Officers, be extra careful when your spouse is sharing and *try* and turn off the judgement filter.

When someone expresses empathy, we feel connection.

INTIMACY TAKES COURAGE

As a law enforcement couple, you probably spend quite a bit of time away from each other. Yes, you may be able to connect through texting or a video chat app, but the deep connection your body and brain wants/needs is different from the soundbites you are able to get. Real intimacy takes the courage to get emotionally vulnerable with each other and the skill of empathy to connect. When you get honest with yourself, your joy and your pain, and share them with your partner, it creates connection. It cannot be a one way street. Both spouses and officers benefit from sharing *and* supporting. It is a gift we give each other. Remembering that we are in the journey together, the struggles and the celebrations. We have each other's *six*.

SO NOW WHAT?

I had a couple in my office for their first session. They had been to counseling before but quit because they felt like their counselor didn't understand the world of law enforcement and the impact it had on the relationship. He was an officer for over ten years when they met, and they had been together for about three years. At the end of our first session, I asked them if they had read Emotional Survival for Law Enforcement. He laughed and said he thought that book was in his desk drawer at work. She had never heard of it. I gave them the book for homework.

The next session, they told me proudly they had read the book. She then stated that she didn't know if she could stay in the relationship if the book represented the life that was in the future for them. She was upset by the book and leaning toward hopeless. It was a different reaction than what I had which was complete joy at finally figuring out what the hell was going on with the guy that I met. I had been with him through this law enforcement journey. I knew what he had inside of him at his core. She did not know her partner prior to the impact of law enforcement and thus, it was hard to have hope.

If you are a spouse reading this, you might be thinking the same way. You both might be saying, "Cyndi, what the literal F*** right now! Basically, you are saying we are doomed!" I hope you aren't but in case you are, I would ***not*** have bothered to write this if I didn't have some answers. Officers, your job may impact your brain and the way you see the world, but you do not have to be a victim to it. You can *choose* to work and operate differently. You, as a couple, cannot be a victim and statistic to law enforcement.

From here forward, we are only talking about solutions. I have provided some of those already. Some of you might read between the lines on others.

I think it is important to know what is lurking under the surface. Hopefully, you now understand what is potentially lurking under the surface from both of your perspectives. You also have some framework or idea of what it takes to have a connected relationship that can overcome and thrive despite the impact and time apart. We do not stop growing as people. We continue to experience events that happen around us and involve us. Your relationship is a living organism and must shift and grow as you go through your life. We must pay attention and tend to the small cuts prior to them becoming infected or prior to there being multiple wounds. You must be willing to stand in each other's shoes and understand their world.

THE SHOES

In my early 20's, I worked as a waitress as a side hustle in order to pay for graduate school. I didn't have much money, so I bought shoes at discount shoe stores. I went to work thinking the shoes would serve their purpose. They did. They also caused me to slide on the wet floor in the kitchen and fall. I knew I needed to get different shoes that would allow me to work safely on the job.

When I got my first professional job, my boss told me that shoes said a lot about a person and I needed to clean mine up. I remember my dad shining my dress shoes as a kid. I took this advice and started making sure the shoes I had were clean and polished in the back where the shoe met the mat of my car.

When I met my husband, I was working at a non-profit. I taught workshops a lot and I would go home complaining about my feet. He told me that it was my shoes and it was time to invest in quality shoes rather than ones that were just cute. He was right. My feet and my back stopped hurting.

Although my husband might argue with me, I don't consider myself a "shoe person."". I am a shoe person when it comes to looking at other people's shoes. I see women wear shoes that I am not sure I could walk in. I bought a pair that my business partner told me were, "super comfortable" and they hurt just sitting in my therapy chair. Nope. No thank you. Don't get me wrong, I wear heels to my office quite a bit. I like how I feel just a little more professional wearing them. They tend to make me feel confident. (And I find some good deals on the sale rack!)

My husband wears the same pair of shoes to work every day. I bet you can guess what they look like and the color. We've bought various brands trying to find what pair of black boots are best for his feet. We have learned to look for a side zipper because lacing all the way up every day is a pain and a waste of time when it's the middle of the night and you are getting called out to a scene. Ironically, his casual travel shoes are a tan version of the shoe. Yes, he has flip flops, cowboy boots, sneakers, and dress shoes. When I think of him in shoes, it's the boots I think of.

One day, I was sitting in my chair talking with a client and I happened to look down at his shoes. He was wearing casual slip-on loafers of some kind. I'm sure they have a name but I'm not in the loop. I just quietly thought to myself, "uh..." and noticed what I felt inside. I got home that night and hugged my husband and told him, "I don't think I could be married to a guy who wears loafers everyday." He just laughed.

To me, there is something about his shoes. The wear and tear. The dirt and ... huh... grime. The way he keeps them polished despite their age. His shoes are a reminder to me of what he does. I sometimes hate those shoes and think they are ugly. Then I have respect for the shoes. I think about how they have been with my husband shift after shift. He changes his uniform, socks, and underwear, but the shoes are there every day. I'm not.

There is an old saying about walking a mile in a person's shoes. I also think about the saying, "if these walls could talk." I started thinking about wearing my husband's shoes and what the shoes would say, if they could talk and all the things that I would learn. It took me over half our relationship to figure out what we needed from each other.

We needed to stand in each other's shoes.

PERSPECTIVE TAKING

What we want most is to be understood by someone. When someone tries to walk in our shoes, they try to understand that we experience and what we feel. They may not get it perfectly. The attempt of knowing deeply, connects us.

Let me get "woo-woo" for a little bit. Take a couple of minutes and think of standing in your spouse's shoes.

What do you think they experience throughout the day?

Who do they talk to?

Who do they want to avoid?

What are they doing?

How do they feel going through their day?

What are their frustrations?

What do they laugh about?

What do they dread?

What gives them the perk to keep going?

It's important to realize that this is what you *think* they are experiencing. Unless you have asked about these things in the last week, you are making an educated guess based upon your experience with your spouse or you are just assuming.

Now, take a couple more minutes and think about standing in your spouse's shoes and what they are experiencing with you?

What has their interaction been like with you?

How do they feel when they see you?

How has love and caring been demonstrated to them?

How have they felt understood?

What are their frustrations?

What do they laugh about?

What do they dread?

What keeps them going?

What do they believe you think or feel about them?

Obviously, we cannot always know what it is like to stand in each other's shoes. We do the best we can. We use our knowledge of what we *think* their world includes. Based upon our interaction with them, we can try to think like they do or how we think they may think. We may use past or current information. We also apply our own interpretations and assumptions from our lives to theirs. We create narrative or stories around information that we don't have. The fact is that as a law enforcement couple, we often spend much of our time apart either due to shifts or sleeping. Much of the time we do not really *know* what is happening in the other person's world. We don't really understand what is going on or the emotional impact from it. Our brain fills in the gaps when we don't have information. Our brains create a story.

I spend a lot of time working with couples that hide information from each other. They are usually in my office because something is not working in their relationship. I hear a lot of clever and creative ways that people hide behavior and fool their partner. Your brain is obviously influenced by the experiences that it has. Just like my husband's brain is influenced, so is mine. I will have moments of distrust in our relationship. He has never given me a reason to distrust, but my brain will start making up stories about different behaviors.

Several years into our relationship, I noticed that we weren't cuddling as much, being physically loving, or having sex as often. Nevermind that we were both experiencing stress from our job and not seeing each other much because of schedules. *My* brain started getting suspicious. First, it attacked me. I started thinking that I'm not as attractive as I used to be to him. Maybe I needed to do something else. Perhaps something was wrong with me. Soon after, my brain then started thinking about the time that he spent at work or alone. My brain went on red alert and started thinking he might be talking to someone. I went searching. I looked at this phone, and there weren't any text messages. What the hell! Who deletes their text messages?

People that want to hide information, that's who! Ahhhhhh! So, he WAS hiding something from me. History. History. How do I get to his search history? What would he be searching on? What about his emails? My brain started spinning. It created a whole story of how he was hiding a relationship from me, and the entire reason we weren't having intimacy is that he was doin' it with someone else, even if it's just some online relationship! Sneaky bastard!

I went on the offense and said something like, "I saw you deleted all your text messages. What are you hiding?"

I remember his face, so confused, and he said, "What?" I explained my research and deep-dive investigation.

He then told me, "Honey. You know the department pays for my phone, right?"

Me: "Yeah"

Him: "You realize that anything on my phone is searchable and public record, right?"

Me: "Oh. I guess, yeah."

Him: "First, do you really think I would do anything to jeopardize my career?"

Me: "No, you like it too much."

Him: "Right. Second, do you really think I have the time or the energy to do what you are suggesting?"

Me: "Probably not, but you never know!"

Him: "Third, you know I don't like clutter. I delete everything."

Me: Defeated and feeling stupid. "Ok, fine. I just miss you, and it sucks we don't get to be with each other."

I have to give my husband a lot of credit. He did not blow up on me at all. That whole conversation could have gone really wrong. He could have become defensive and attacked back. He knows my head messes with me at times, and I appreciate him walking through it. There are times now, after a tough or twisted session with a couple, that I will call him and say things like, “If you are going to cheat on me, don’t tell me and just leave me first, please!” His response is almost always, “I love you. Tough session, eh?”

STORIES WE TELL OURSELVES.

Stories are impacted by the way we see the world and our relationships.

Our brains are wired for story. They can also be called “narratives.” When I talk about the story or narrative that we create, some people think I am telling them they are “making up a story” as in lying. That is *not* what I am saying here. Our brain strings together events and interprets behaviors and interactions based upon the narrative or story of your life. This is why we can experience the same event with a group of people, but we all experience it in a different way. It’s why witnesses of an accident will have different stories. Well, that and they may be lying. Or, maybe that’s my story.

Your personal experiences impact the stories that your brain creates; events in your life, values, beliefs, and interactions, to name a few. From all of our experiences, our brain learns. Just like in school, your brain picks up on "lessons" it needs to learn from interactions and events. It is helpful to take time to determine the lessons you have learned and if there is a common theme to those lessons. As in the example above, if your brain is exposed to people that lie, cheat, and steal all the time, your brain will pick up on that experience as a lesson and then apply the overarching theme of "People are deceitful. Watch out." These themes get applied to your brain when information is missing, but also because our brain is wired to protect us.

One of the most common that I hear is, "you can't trust people," which I think is very relevant to a lifestyle in law enforcement.

There may be themes in your stories that apply to other people, such as, "Everyone has an angle," "People are just out for themselves," or "People don't care what I think. They are just nice." You may be able to relate to these and probably have some others. Not every theme is negative. There can be positive themes such as "If I am honest and work hard, others will respect me," "Family takes care of their own," or "I can overcome hard things." Being aware of some of your common themes will help you to pause when you come across them.

As I mentioned, the brain likes to create stories. Unfortunately, many times it is creating a story in order to determine whether or not it needs to protect us from danger or react. We then wind up reacting to the story. Knowing our themes are helpful but you need to go a step further and reality check the theme with that person. You have to be in charge of the story.

When you have identified the story or narrative that you are creating in a situation, take a moment and think about what you know about this person. Let's say the story you are creating is that this person, in this case your spouse, has an "angle". Your brain thinks they are doing or saying something for their own good or benefit. Fact check this. Think about what you know about this person, their character, and their intentions. Has this person done that in the past? Thinking about the history that you have with a person can help to determine if this is a fact or a story that your brain is creating for you.

Stories are impacted by the way we see the world and our relationships. In a previous chapter, I discussed Drs. Gottman's Sound Relationship House. An important element of The House that applies to the story is the Positive Perspective. When you have a positive perspective on your relationship or with the people which you are interacting with, you have the potential to have a positive story. The Positive Perspective is an important element of your relationship if you want to ensure that negative stories are not impacting your relationship. It is a struggle for many in law enforcement due to exposure to so many negative elements on a daily basis.

LOOK AT YOUR SHOES

Be aware of the "shoes" that you wear. Of course, I don't mean your literal shoes. I am talking figuratively. Your shoes are referring to the journey of your life. Take a minute and think about what your shoes would look like.

Are you aware of the scuffs, wear, tears, grime, and grit?

Have you paid attention to their condition?

Is your big toe sticking out?

Have you kept them polished and clean?

Do they stink?

Are you proud of these shoes?

No one goes through life unscathed. We all have wear and tear on our shoes. What is important is to determine if we have just continually adapted to the poor condition of the shoes or if we have taken time to repair them and get them in better condition. When we do not examine how our journey impacts the way we think and feel. The shoes, or our journey, starts causing us pain and injury to ourselves and those around us. It impacts the way we see and interact with the world. We have the ability to stop and determine if there is a repair to make or an adjustment to decrease the impact. Are you wearing a pair of beat up stinky shoes in your relationship? And no, you can't just go buy new shoes.

GET CURIOUS ABOUT YOUR PARTNER'S SHOES

Early in our relationship, we are most curious about our partner's world and the shoes they stand in. As we go along in our relationship, we sometimes stop being so curious. There could be several reasons for this including "life" happening, not seeing each other, being tired, or a lack of engagement or response from our spouse. For whatever reason, we either stop sharing the little bits of our life, stop getting curious about little bits in our partner's life, or our partner stops sharing for some reason. Get curious about their story and their shoes.

This sounds like a simple process, right? Just start getting curious. Remember, I'm asking you to stand in your partner's shoes. Sometimes those shoes pinch, are too big, or you don't appreciate that your partner hasn't taken care of their own shoes.

What I find is that there are a couple of elements that prevent us from being able to be curious.

1. Your brain is too busy thinking about your own shoes and story. You are thinking about what you have to do or what you want to do rather than what is going on in your spouse's world. While this could be that you are not considering others, it could also be that your brain is on overload, tired, or staying in fight or flight. Hard to consider others when you are in self-preservation. If this is something you relate to, start considering ways to unwind so you can be present for your spouse.
2. Time. In a law enforcement relationship, time is typically a luxury. It is essential to your relationship to make time to keep up with your partner's world. Consider talking to your spouse about how you can best make the time even if it is for ten minutes a day. You might even have conversation

around specific elements that are important to your partner.

3. It's difficult to hear emotion. Sometimes standing in your partner's shoes means that you have to listen to difficult situations, pain, or emotion. Maybe your partner expresses their stress in a way that sounds like yelling to you. Maybe your partner is crying and you are uncomfortable with tears. Our bodies can tend to react to this, shut us down, or want to shut our partner down. Taking deep breaths can calm our fight or flight system. Listen for content and emotion rather than the way it is being expressed.
4. Defensiveness. Our brain is too busy hearing things as blame rather than an experience. I see this in officers many times when their spouse is talking about how they feel about overtime or the lack of time they have together. Hear what your partner is saying as a complaint about the situation rather than a criticism of you. We are in this together and it's ok to not be ok about the situation sometimes. Don't personalize it.
5. Criticism. As you listen to your partner's story you judge them for the way they handle things or the way they see the world. You minimize the events in their life. "You are busy doing x and I have to deal with y. What's the big deal?" Recognize that you and your spouse and have different perspectives, experiences, and thresholds. Listen for the pain, acknowledge the feeling, and then ask how you can support rather than criticize.
6. Contempt. I find two aspects of contempt that impact the ability to stand in your partner's shoes. The first is having disdain for your partner. It could be the way they discipline the children, manage their health, see the world, or a variety of other reasons. If this is the case, find a way to have an appreciation that the two of you think differently here. This

> could be another area to dig into and get even more curious, so you understand this aspect of your partner. Maybe there is a story they have yet to share with you. This is how I found out some very interesting stories of my husband's childhood that shaped who he is today. I was able to move some aspects of contempt to compassion and understanding.

The second is having unresolved hurt and pain in the relationship which makes you unavailable to really listen or be there for your spouse. If this is the case, I recommend that you talk to a counselor and get help as a couple to move through the pain.

As you get curious about your partner's world, be aware if you are having a reaction or a resistance to listening or the information your spouse is sharing. Get *more* curious when those shoes are pinching rather than creating story and reacting.

Yes, it can suck sometimes

Emotional vulnerability can get in the way of listening to any of our spouse's stories in a law enforcement relationship. As we spoke about in the previous chapter, it takes courage and vulnerability to be in any relationship much less this one.

Be aware of the biases you have about your spouse. What are your biases? Do you see them as brave, unaffected, strong, weak, emotional, tender, or some other way? Sometimes we work to see our spouse in a certain way because *we* need them to be that way.

I have had several conversations with officer spouses that feel very uncomfortable when their officer expresses emotion or insecurity. They want their officer to be their "Knight" and they work to keep them on their horse by dismissing the officers attempt to share or trying to fix the situation. I was not immune from this and found myself in this situation the first time my husband told me he was struggling. On the outside I was listening, providing empathy, and support. On the inside I was freaking out a little.

I realized it was uncomfortable to see my husband in this vulnerable place and my brain wanted to shut it down or run away. I know there is a strong part of my journey and story that needs to feel protected by my husband. My brain saw that as being threatened as he was vulnerable.

As an officer's spouse, it is normal to struggle to hear what your spouse experiences and sees on the job. There have been times when tears rolled down my face as I listened to stories from my husband. It is ok for you to allow yourself to feel those emotions. Be careful of reacting with your words or facial expressions. You want your officer to be able to turn toward or lean into you when they are struggling. You have to be ok listening to some hard stuff sometimes.

The first scene my husband shared with me was tough to hear as he shared details of the condition of the man who had shot himself, what he saw, smelled, heard, and his thoughts in that moment. I can picture the scene as the description he gave me was detailed and created an image in my mind. (Thanks, brain!) I remember listening but my brain said, "Stop!" I knew he needed to share it, so I didn't. If this happens to you, take some deep breaths. Focus on what it was like for your officer and just listen. It's ok if you need to talk about it later but do it with a safe friend who gets your world.

> ***You are not burdening your spouse by sharing!***

As an officer, it is often hard to hear how the job impacts your spouse whether it is worry, anxiety, feeling like a single parent much of the time, or how the house runs one way when you are at work and another when you are home. You are not being blamed. It is not always yours to fix. Sometimes you just need to listen and tell your spouse that you "get it" and it "sucks." Second, **YOU ARE NOT BURDENING YOUR SPOUSE BY SHARING**! It is ok that you want to protect your family and loved ones from what you experience every day. That is honorable. It is not healthy!

It is also not fair to your spouse! It communicates that you think less of them. You are saying, "I can be there for you and support you, but I don't think you are good enough or strong enough to support me." That is not kind. It is emotionally vulnerable for you to allow your spouse to be there for you. It is also *allowing them* to love you in the way that you love them. Stop stuffing and start sharing!

STANDING IN THEIR SHOES IMPROVES CONNECTION

When you work to stand in your spouse's shoes and understand their world, it is easier to maintain the connection that you want and need as a couple. Much of the time, we lack the natural opportunity for connection through daily [1]rituals of "good morning," "good-bye," dinner times, and weekends.

We must purposefully work to stay connected. Here are some ways that standing in each other's shoes can impact connection.

Meaningful gestures: People often show love in the way that they want to express it rather than thinking like their partner. Thinking of what gestures are meaningful to your partner can create connection in little ways.

Example: My husband knows that I am almost always running late and therefore makes extra coffee to leave me in the pot in the morning to make my life easier.

Support your spouse emotionally: By standing in their shoes, you understand their emotions or how they may react to situations. You know them so well you can think about what they are experiencing. Reach out to them and be specific with your emotional support.

Example: I know working a day shift is more stressful than working a night shift. I may reach out during the day and say, "I hope admin is leaving you alone to get your shit done. I know it stresses you out. Looking forward to sitting on our porch in a couple of days, sharing wine, and venting."

Reduce reaction to an emotional situation: You can consider what your spouse may be going through and see through their eyes. When you listen and respond to the feeling, it makes your spouse feel heard and connects them to you. Review information on empathy in the earlier chapter if you need to.

Example: An officer listens to the spouses story about how the kids acted up all day, how they feel alone in dealing with the situation, and like a single parent and responds, "I can hear how exhausted, alone, and frustrated you are. It sucks for sure."

Make difficult conversation easier: If we take time to stand in our spouse's shoes and think about how they want to hear the difficult information, it makes our approach more kind. We may also recognize that the information we want to share is a criticism rather than something helpful.

Example: Instead of saying, "Why the hell did you do that?" I think through how my husband would receive that and instead say, "I'm confused as to what led you to do that. Can you help me understand?"

De-escalate a difficult conversation: Our brains are wired to protect us in difficult conversation. By working to stand in the other person's shoes, we can listen to where they are coming from and hear their point of view. We stay out of defensiveness. If both partners can do this, the conversation can become about problem solving rather than defending our behavior.

Work together what stories and narratives are harmful to your relationship:. Sometimes in standing in each other's shoes, we realize that we think or see the world differently, have different goals, or visions for the future. When we get curious and work to understand each other, we can work together to change them.

Example: When my husband is off, I want to *go* and have a new experience with him. He wants to stay at the house. In working to understand each other, he understood that I wanted to play and the importance of it. I understood that his brain starts stressing about who is going to run into and "turn on" rather than powering down and relaxing. We work together to find ways that satisfy us both rather than one person giving in to what the other wants.

Have awareness of how law enforcement culture and lifestyle impacts: When we really stand in each other's shoes, we are able to understand the potential impact law enforcement culture has on each other. We can then work as a team to mitigate the impact. More of which you will learn in the next chapter.

Help your spouse out by communicating your story. Your spouse cannot read your mind and most of us do not like to be bombarded with questions or dig to get story updates. Make sure that you are sharing what is going on in your day. Share both information, emotion (positive and negative), and challenges. Share in soundbites and storytelling.

Check in with soundbytes when away from each other by texting or making a note to others, "remind me about (topic)" or "X just happened and I'm so excited. Remind me to tell you!" Follow up with storytelling when you both have emotional energy and time.

Communicate your story. If you don't want a bunch of questions, you need to start sharing your story.

PHRASES THAT ARE HELPFUL

There are several phrases I find helpful when standing in your partner's shoes, especially when you really don't understand something. Try to stay out of using the word "why" as it almost always puts people on the defensive. Here are a few phrases to use:

- Tell me more about......
- Can you help me understand....
- What I hear you saying is....
- That sounds like it would feel.....
- The story I hear you have about that is...
- The story I am telling myself about what you are saying is....
- I'm confused. Can you help me .....
- I'm thinking that must have been __________ for you.

Hopefully, you can use some of these phrases to get curious about the way each other is thinking and feeling.

As we work to understand that our partner's world and shoes are different than ours, we start to connect more intimately with who they are. We feel seen when our partner does this for us, and they feel the same. There is an added layer to consider when it comes to the impact of law enforcement for both the officer *and* the spouse. We are each being impacted and work together to support each other in a connected way.

HEROES DON'T DO IT ALONE®

When I decided that I wanted to share what I had learned about Law Enforcement and our relationships, I wanted to make sure that officers and spouses knew that they were not "in it" alone. That ultimately, both partners are "in it." Both sacrifice in different ways and both have the potential to have their mental health impacted. Together can be better. Knowing that we are going through the journey together, sometimes makes it easier. My tag line for Code4Couples® became Heroes Don't Do It Alone®.

I'm not a superhero fanatic. I just know the basics so you may be able to prove me wrong on this point. When I think about the superheroes I know, none of them go at it alone. Some of them have sidekicks while fighting crime and others support them emotionally. Batman wound up having both a sidekick in Robin and the emotional support in Alfred. Superman had Lois Lane.

Even the emotionally aloof Tony Stark has Jarvis (ok, he's a robot) and Pepper Potts to connect with and confide in. Every superhero I know also has some kind of internal conflict or trauma they have endured. *None* of them are perfect. Batman's parents were murdered, and he is basically a vigilante trying to heal an old wound.

Superman's parents saved him, unable to save themselves, and he constantly felt like he didn't belong as he grew up. Tony Stark has "daddy issues!" They aren't perfect. They have a small group of people around them that they trust and lean on. They also made the decision that they would not be a victim to their situation or circumstances. They were resilient. We need to be the same.

In the last chapter, I emphasized the importance of understanding the world you live in as well as your spouse's using my shoe analogy. You will be impacted in a variety of ways in your life including law enforcement. One of the best ways to thrive through a career in law enforcement is to have a meaningful relationship. You need to learn to be resilient both individually and as a couple.

RESILIENCE

When I ask people what they think about resilience, the most common answer I get is "bouncing back." When I hear that, I think of my brother's Stretch Armstrong. I am going to assume most of you did *not* have a Stretch Armstrong and describe it to you. "Stretch" was an 18-inch toy man that had legs and arms that you could stretch and stretch and when you released them, they went back into shape. We aren't "Stretch." When things happen to us, we change in some way.

Resilience is the ability to recover from or adjust easily to misfortune or change. Every event is different and adjusting to some events may take more time than other events. The key is the *ability* to adjust. It sometimes takes time to adapt to a new normal. Sometimes our body can adapt easily, sometimes it adapts begrudgingly, and sometimes it just doesn't adapt.

Mental Health Impact

We talked earlier in the book about small doses of poison that officers ingest daily when they go to work. Spouses can also ingest the poison if they are experiencing secondary trauma or anxiety. I also shared the frog in the pot analogy where the frog is unaware of what is happening in its environment and just continually adjusting to the increased heat until it is too late for it to use its legs to jump out and save itself. Don't be the frog. If you need a more entertaining and disgusting version, find "Frog in the Blender." I use the video in my presentations with officers and spouses. It is memorable. Don't be the frog.

There is a lot of conversation around suicide and PTSD. The [1]facts show that the majority of officers do not develop mental health disorders as a part of the career. [2]This is continuing to be impacted positively due to awareness of issues and officers wanting to have healthier lifestyles. "Statistically, police officers are on par with or, in some instances slightly above the general population in terms of rates of mental health issues."

Wouldn't it be great to have some sort of indication that would throw up flags far in advance to prevent the slippery slope of all the elements we have talked about thus far? There is! It's called Compassion Satisfaction. Compassion Satisfaction is the satisfaction that professionals experience when helping traumatized individuals. In other words, after I go to the call, did I, as an officer, feel like I was making a difference and feel satisfied? Overall, individuals become officers because they truly want to serve and protect. My husband will also argue that it is also to kick ass on occasion. I know he got into the field because he was willing to step into situations that others would not or could not. He enjoys watching out and protecting his family and they appreciate, most of the time, when he does so. I appreciate it too... most of the time.

I have been in the world of policing a while now. Things have changed. There is a constant video and public eye on them. They are asked to protect but criticized when they are doing their job. There are departments that have little to no support. Spouses that need to be careful about who they are around or what they say. Officers are being scrutinized, belittled, shamed, and generally feel unsafe. Spouses also feel unsafe and worried. At one time, as a law enforcement couple, we reconciled the sacrifice with the service provided to the community. Many times, that community turns against those who serve them. We are all tired.

In a 2019 research [3]article, the authors discuss the impact on officers. The research found that close to 40% of officers surveyed had low levels of Compassion Satisfaction. "This percentage suggests that almost half of the surveyed officers did not experience their role as police officers in a way that gave them job satisfaction. The findings also revealed that a considerable number of study participants did not feel satisfied by helping those who suffer, or that they were not able to appreciate the value of their important work." *Almost half*! By the way, 32% of officers indicated they had moderate Compassion Satisfaction and 10% with high Compassion Satisfaction. Another interesting part of this study is that years of service had *nothing* to do with Compassion Satisfaction. That floored me. My assumption was that it would come in age like the cynicism that Dr. Martin talks about in his book.

There are many jobs where people don't feel valued or appreciated. That's not what this is addressing. The term Compassion Satisfaction targets those occupations that deal with people in trauma and crisis. These would include other first responders, medical personnel, and mental health professionals. My husband sent me a text today with an image. He wrote "truth" and the image said, "Nobody loves the warrior until the enemy is at the gate." We live the life. We know what is happening, the feelings, and emotions. We as a couple have to prevent our own low "Compassion Satisfaction" from spilling over into our relationship with each other.

A positive aspect of this study is that addressing the Compassion Satisfaction positively impacts the officer's mental health and resilience. If we address the Compassion Satisfaction, we prevent compassion fatigue, which makes officers more susceptible to other mental health issues. We can be a victim, or we can be resilient.

My husband thinks of resilience as weapon maintenance. He does actions daily to make sure that his weapon will function in the manner that he wants it to function. This includes wiping it off from dust if it needs it and ensuring that he has a bullet in the chamber prior to going to work. He checks the light mounted on the frame. I know this because it's bright at 6am. He performs other tasks on a weekly basis such as examining his magazines which may include loading and reloading his bullets and wiping it down more completely. Every couple of weeks he breaks it down and cleans it completely making sure to lubricate it. He is known for having a clean weapon that always functions because of his diligence. He says that resilience is just like weapon maintenance. Whether you are addressing your personal resilience or your resilience as a couple, the same principles can be applied.

RESILIENT THINKING

When we resist our present reality, it causes problems. People get stuck in adapting and it causes problems in their own mental health, their joy, and their relationships. I'm sure you can think of situations where you had to adapt in your relationship either due to law enforcement or not. You have probably had to adapt to change holidays, plans, schedules, goals, dreams, or numerous other situations. When we struggle to adapt, we get stuck in the grieving process. Instead of moving through, we think or say, "This isn't fair" or "Why me?" These are key signs you are having a resilience issue related to your mindset which impacts not only our individual lives but our relationship.

Whether you are addressing your personal resilience or your resilience as a couple, the same principles can be applied.

Locus of Control

There is a key element that comes up over and over again when I interview people for my podcast who understand what it takes to move through law enforcement life successfully as an individual or a couple. Many of these people have fallen and had to figure out what happened after their fall. It is mentioned in Dr. Gilmartin's book and even came up during my interview with Lt. Col. Grossman. What I hear is that there is a mindset that must switch in officers and spouses. That switch is moving away from a victim mentality to the life of law enforcement. They don't name it, but they are saying exactly what I know is the psychological concept of Locus of Control by Julian Rotter.

Locus of Control refers to how strongly people believe they have control over the situations and experiences that affect their lives. I like to tell people it's the difference between, "Life happens to me" or "I make life happen." When events or situations happen or sometimes don't happen in our life our adjustment or resilience is affected by our mindset and locus of control. An external locus of control means that life is happening to me. It can result in us feeling stuck, angry, resentful, depressed, anxious, and lead us to making emotional decisions or using negative coping skills. An internal locus of control means that life happens, and I make decisions on how I will adapt and change. An external locus of control often results in a reaction while an internal locus of control results in a response.

This is particularly important in law enforcement where officers often feel they do not have control of what they get to do on a daily basis and where spouses do not feel like they have much control due to the department taking priority. It feels as if the department and citizens control time, schedules, energy, and much more. It is easy to fall into the trap of feeling victimized by the department or career. When we do, it damages our well-being and our ability to connect in a positive way as a couple. We cannot hold the department accountable, so we blame our officer or spouse for the lack of understanding. We start attacking each other rather than coming together and figuring out how to not let it impact our relationship and connection.

THINKING ERRORS

So, if I know my audience, I'm guessing you do not want to be a victim to the world, and you are ready to develop or strengthen your internal locus of control. This doesn't just apply to the impact of law enforcement but also your relationship. A challenge to your internal locus of control is your brain. The brain, again, in its goals to keep you safe and not make you happy, has a habit of interpreting situations negatively. You are wired for survival and that is the road your brain naturally takes you down which almost emphasizes the powerlessness felt in an external locus of control. Thanks a lot, *brain*! In short, your brain lies to you and it's important to check for lies!

These thinking errors are a part of a therapy called Cognitive Behavioral Therapy (CBT) founded by Dr. Aaron Beck. These thinking errors are found to be the most popular and cause errors in decision making, reactions, and create anxiety and depression. As you read through them, consider what ones your brain tends to implement.

. . .

Black and White Thinking or All or Nothing Thinking

As the name implies, there is one choice or another. There is no middle ground or gray here! Things are all good or all bad. In law enforcement, this is very popular as it keeps a distinct line between right and wrong or legal and illegal.

Examples: "*If I'm not perfect, I have failed*" or "*I do it right or not at all.*"

Overgeneralization

Overgeneralization is seeing a single event as a never-ending pattern or overly broad in the conclusions we make. It can apply to a group of people or an event.

Examples: "*You NEVER listen to me,*" "*Nothing good EVER happens,*" "*People are ALWAYS going to look out for themselves,*" or "*That steak tasted awful. I'm never having steak again.*"

Mental Filter

A mental filter is when someone is only paying attention to placing emphasis on certain information that may validate a negative belief. You pick out a single negative detail and dwell on it exclusively so that your vision of all reality becomes darkened.

Examples: You focus on the 10% you struggle with rather than the 90% you are successful with or have improved.

You believe that your wife is a nag, and you filter in all the negative comments rather than also hearing the appreciation or positive comments made.

Disqualifying the Positive

Discounting or dismissing positive comments or events. You reject positive experiences by insisting that they don't count. This thinking takes the joy out of life and makes you feel inadequate, less than, and unrewarded.

Examples: "*They are just saying that to be nice.*" "*It wasn't my leadership; it was the team that did the work,*" "*It was just luck,*" or "*Yeah, I was able to help most of those people, but what about the two I couldn't.*"

Jumping to Conclusions

Jumping to Conclusions is when we interpret things negatively when there are no facts to support a conclusion. There are two types. Mind Reading is imaging what others are thinking and concluding that someone is reacting to you negatively. Fortune Telling is predicting a negative future and how it will turn out badly.

Examples: "She may say that she finds me sexy, but I know she thinks I need to lose weight." "I know if I don't lose weight, she isn't going to find me sexy, and she is going to leave me." "I see them over there talking and laughing. I bet they are talking about me."

Catastrophizing

Believing things are far worse than they are, blowing things out of proportion, or minimizing something to make it seem less important. This thinking has two parts. First, predicting a negative outcome, and second, jumping to the conclusion that it would be catastrophic if the negative outcome were true.

Example: "He's *not returning my call. He's probably ignoring me. Maybe he is talking to that new dispatcher. What if they have a connection and he realizes that I am not what he wants and needs. He will wind up leaving me, and how will I support myself and the kids. There is no way I can make it on one salary. He would fight me on child support. What an asshole that he wants me to be alone!*" "*I could have done better on that call. I am sure no one will trust me now, and my career may be over.*"

. . .

Emotional Reasoning

We are assuming something must be true because we think or feel a certain way. A person concludes that something is true based upon their emotional reaction. Emotions can skew your thoughts, but those skewed thoughts become a reality.

Example: "*I feel selfish (bad/guilty) about saying no to overtime. I am so selfish.*" "*I am embarrassed I said that. I am an idiot.*" "*I am worthless for not being able to save that person. I'm sure that my family and the department think I'm worthless as well.*"

Shoulding & Musting

Therapists commonly say, "Stop shoulding on yourself" or "quit musterbating." The words "should," "ought," and "must" are words we use to shame ourselves or others and put unreasonable demands on ourselves even though, at times, they are helpful and necessary. These words are often applied to other people when we do not like behavior. We "should" on ourselves. Sometimes these words are used to motivate ourselves to do something, and when we do not, they equate to shame and negative feelings.

Example: "*I shouldn't have eaten those fries!*" "*I should get things right the first time.*" "*I must never go to bed angry.*"

Labeling

Labeling is an extreme form of all or nothing thinking. It can be that a characteristic of a person is generalized and assigned to the whole person. Instead of labeling a behavior, we label the entire person.

Example: Someone makes a rude comment or challenges you, and you think, "*They are just an asshole!*" or "*I waited until the last minute. I am so lazy.*"

. . .

Personalization and Blame

Personalization occurs when you hold yourself personally responsible for an event that was not entirely under your control; it could also result in "magical thinking" that it would have changed the course of events if you had done something differently. Blame is when individuals blame others or their circumstances for their problems and overlook how they may be contributing to the situation. The result of this can come out as entitlement or victimization.

Examples: "*If I had been faster, those people would have lived,*" "*If I weren't gone all the time, we would have a better relationship,*" "*I do everything right, and they always look past me for promotion,*" "It's *all my fault,*" or "*I had nothing to do with this.*"

I am sure that some of those sounded familiar to you. When we are dealing with a situation, especially a negative or emotionally vulnerable situation, our brain tends to implement one of these thinking errors. Recognize the thinking error and work to change the belief to something more accurate and positive. Check out facts if you need help with changing the belief.

GRATITUDE

A note about gratitude here: gratitude is a large part of a resilient mind. It combats the negative filters and views that people with crappy people in crappy situations can cause. It can also combat foreboding joy as mentioned in the previous chapter. Gratitude is an action and not just a mindset or an attitude. Gratitude allows us to find purpose or appreciation. When you find yourself struggling with a negative mindset, think of something you are grateful to have in your life. It is not about finding a silver lining. It is finding some time for which to be grateful. It can truly be anything. In those moments when you feel down or negative, stop and reframe your thinking to gratitude. Have gratitude check-ins with each other. You can text "gratitude check" to one other and respond with a gratitude you have in the moment.

RELATIONSHIP COMPASS

Resilience in an action and a continual process of assessing and acting. You must assess yourself, look at your own shoes and their condition, as well as the relationship. Focus on changing behaviors and beliefs that assist your resilience and continually course correct.

Many resilience models include officers having a personal moral compass. Dr. Stephanie Conn [4]says, "Having a personal moral compass means that our commitment to and participation in activities are guided by intentionality." The idea of a compass is also addressed in the Sound Relationship Model by Drs. Gottman, "Making Life Dreams and Aspirations Come True", intentional behavior to help partners achieve the dreams they have for their life including play, fun, exploration, and adventure as well as "Creating Shared Meaning", intentionally prioritizing and utilizing the couple's time and resources to create meaning, history, and legacy.

Having a relationship compass means that you are committed to participating in activities including the utilization of time and resources that intentionally support you and your partner's life dreams, meaning, history, and legacy. When considering aspects of your compass, you might also want to consider mind, body, and spirit, nurturing these elements in regard to your relationship. Here are some examples of what I mean:

Mind: Mentally healthy, positive mindset, thinking positively of the relationship, continually growing and learning, engaging each other in deeper meaningful conversation, learning a new hobby or language, developing a creative plan for a new house or outdoor area, etc.

Body: Physical health, exercise, weight, sleep, sex, minimizing impact on the job or recovering from an injury in order to do something in the future, eating foods that support a longer life, addressing issues from the job such as blood pressure and cholesterol, etc.

Spirit: Spirituality, values, beliefs, nurturing your soul in a world that seems all bad, seeing the good in humanity or creating good, spending time in nature, music, creativity, arts, laughing, friends, etc.

A relationship compass needs to be agreed upon by both partners and continually revisited to ensure that your relationship is staying on course or determining if there needs to be adjustments. Remember that the compass is a way for you as a couple to determine how you want to utilize your time and resources. This helps when it comes to down time and the intentions you set. A compass is you having an internal locus on control in a world that could knock you off course.

Let me give you a simple example of how this might work.

One of the elements of your relationship compass is having a positive perspective with each other and the relationship. This means that if you are feeling negatively that you speak directly to your spouse and discuss the situation. At work, a co-worker notices that you are quiet and confronts you. You briefly share your dissatisfaction in a situation. The co-worker says something negative about their spouse and you soon realize you are spouse bashing. It felt good to have someone to talk to who understands. You start to talk more to this co-worker who then encourages you to go out for drinks to talk more. You realize this is a time that you could spend with your spouse but instead go out for drinks. What's the big deal?

It is the little actions uncorrected that will continually drive your relationship off course. Feel free to talk with co-workers and have drinks. Be aware of the intentions and the intentions of those you spend time with. Be aware of their beliefs toward your relationship, your spouse, and law enforcement. When we are not feeling positive about our relationship, it is easy to be steered off course.

Note: Go to www.holdthelinebook.com and download a Relationship SWOT Analysis and a Relationship Compass Exercise designed to help you take a look at your relationship. The Relationship SWOT Analysis is designed for you to assess the strengths, weaknesses, opportunities and threats in your relationship. The Relationship Compass Exercise will assist you in being focused on those areas of strength and opportunity as well as adjusting the weaknesses and threats.

CONFRONTING OFF-COURSE

There are times when we realize that something is impacting the course of our relationship and we are going to have to confront it. When we are understanding of each other's world and standing in each other's shoes, we need to be able to apply the principle of extending a generous explanation to our spouse's behavior. Drs. Gottman would call this the Positive Perspective.

An example of this would be when my husband comes home and says "hello" to me but not much else. He may be huffing and puffing in frustration and may even snap at me or our 15 year old dog, Gabby. I really want to get after him when he gets after her. That just intensifies things. If you are an officer's spouse, you may have a similar situation in your house and instead of the dog, it's the kids. I've heard about it! Standing in his shoes and understanding his world, a generous explanation and think, "Ok. He's had a crappy day. I don't know what he has been through today or what he has seen. He is tired and probably lacks some capacity to manage those emotions seething through. I know he loves me and loves his dog. He just needs to wind down and I'll give him the space he needs even though he's being a little shit right now. I know he'll come around." That is really what I think.

This can work, for a while, especially when your spouse understands they acted like a shit and took ownership by saying something like, "Sorry I was being an asshole. You didn't deserve that."

Note: Just ignoring the behavior and acting like it didn't happen ***does not work***!

The generous explanation becomes ineffective and damaging when it means that the behavior or belief that needs the generous explanation does not change. If every day you or your spouse comes home and figuratively "kicks the cat," something has to change. If a difficult conversation winds up in shutting down or exploding, something has to change. If every time we ride together, there is some kind of road rage, something has to change. There are going to be times when you have to confront each other. There are boundaries to standing in shoes, understanding each other's world, and providing the generous explanation.

THINK

There is an acronym I love to share (and included in a podcast) that addresses confrontation. I do not claim credit for this nor can I credit where it came from. Before you decide to confront or comment to someone THINK.

Truthful: The statement you are about to make is true. Not an opinion. Not an interpretation. TRUE.

Helpful: This statement is going to be helpful to the person or situation.

Inspiring: The statement will inspire or influence the individual in some way.

Necessary: The words need to be said.

Kind: The statement is kind and said in a kind way.

Sometimes we are wanting to react to what is going on OR maybe we really are unclear about the intention of the behavior we are wanting to address (true). Make sure the confrontation fits before you take the next steps

Clear is Kind

Be succinct and direct as you can regarding what is not working. Say it with kindness. State a feeling if you want. Ask for what you need and want to change. That is confrontation in a nutshell. The hard part is working through all the emotion that you really WANT to take out on your spouse or express. The other hard part is distilling down everything you really WANT to say and getting to the point in a direct, clear, concise manner. Let's use the example above to confront.

"Hey honey, I've noticed that you have been huffing and puffing and snapping at me and the dog the last couple of weeks when you get home.

(It sucks.) Optional

I need to be in the loop of why you're so annoyed rather than being part of what you are annoyed at. Let me know what you think"

OR

"I need you to know whatever is going on is spilling over on to us. I am free to talk about whatever is going on when you are ready."

You notice in this example, I have you getting in and getting out. We aren't going to sit around and talk about it at that moment. I'm going to say what I need to say and then let my partner think about it. Stay away from needing your partner to change such as, "I need you to adjust your tone when you get home."

Let's try another example. You are feeling bossed around by your spouse and criticized for things you are doing.

"Hey hon. I've noticed that when you are letting me know what needs to get done around here that I'm not feeling like part of the team and criticized.

It sucks because I want us to be a team.

I need us to figure out a way to communicate what needs to get done and expectations, so I feel successful. When could we set a time to do that?"

OR

"Hey hon. When you are communicating with me, I am feeling bossed around and criticized.

It sucks.

I need to know from you if you are stressed or if I'm not meeting expectations in some way.

Let's set a time to chat about that."

OR

"Hey Hon. The story I'm telling myself is that you think I'm sucking at something around the house. I need to know if that is true and work together to communicate differently."

Practice finding your voice and what works for you as a couple. You may need to start slowly and be aware of your tone and kindness. Sarcasm never works so stay away from it. There is no perfect way to confront, just a way that works for you. We used to avoid confrontation. Now, we both try to bring things up as they come up so the impact is less and emotions don't fester.

Do not have the expectation that things will be resolved at the moment of confrontation. If you are uncomfortable sitting in the "messy middle" with things unresolved, find a way to mentally have a positive perspective to ease your discomfort or anxiety about the situation. Shifts sometimes make it difficult to resolve situations. You may have to say your peace and schedule a time to talk later.

Instilling a mindset of "we can get through this" is helpful. I shared in a previous chapter that it took several weeks before my husband opened up to share what was going on with him. I kept checking in, not nagging, to let him know, "I see you." Remember the purpose of the confrontation is to keep your relationship on course and your resilience high!

MAKING YOUR RELATIONSHIP CODE 4

At the beginning of this book, I talked about coming up with the name Code4Couples®. We are not always going to be Code 4. Life happens. There will be ups and downs due to life and some of those will be due to the impact of law enforcement. My goal in writing this book is to give you the knowledge, some skills, and ability to have a resilient and Code 4 relationship.

The benefits and impact of having a safe, secure, healthy, connected relationship is immense. It is important for both of you to experience it in order to minimize the impact of a career in law enforcement and thrive afterward.

I see Code4Couples® as:

- Culturally Competent
- Connected
- Compassionate
- Courageous, and
- Counter the Impact

I have talked about all these elements in some way throughout the book but want to bring it all together for you in a clear way. Many of the action steps have questions for you to consider. You can download all the assessment and discussion questions on the website at www.holdthelinebook.com

CULTURALLY COMPETENT

Cultural competence involves the element of knowing and understanding not only the obvious ways the job can impact, such as not seeing and spending time together and sleep, but the unseen and psychological elements such as the OODA loop, hypervigilance, cynicism, and conditioning that occurs. It is also understanding the commitment and impact on the spouse including loneliness, grief from the life they imagined, struggles with family, anxiety, or secondary trauma. Cultural competency refers to what you experience and what your spouse may be experiencing.

It is understanding that the culture of law enforcement impacts the culture of your relationship if you are unaware. Much of what I have written is dedicated to understanding the culture of your relationship and the potential impact on aspects of your relationship. It's time to determine what you are going to do about it.

I have to admit that initially when I read about the potential impact, I thought I just needed to accommodate. That this gave my husband permission to act and behave. "Poor him. Poor me." That is a *victim* mentality! It is not an excuse for behavior but a call to action to address the impact. Code4Couples® become knowledgeable and then adjust to an internal locus of control and are resilient.

ACTION STEPS:

Assess

1. Think about who you were prior to law enforcement entering your life. Consider how you connected with people, your mindset, your mental health, your beliefs, activities, and hobbies.
2. Think about who you are now and consider those same elements.
3. Do the same thing for your partner.
4. Think about the goals and dreams you had at the beginning of the relationship and consider where you are now.
5. Looking at the changes or difference, what could be contributed to spillover from law enforcement?

Discuss

1. Talk with your spouse about your findings or insights you have about yourself.
2. Ask your partner to share their insights about you. What insights are similar? What is different? What is difficult to hear? Do not defend. Just listen and take in the information.
3. Get clarity. Are there things said that you need more information about? Is there additional feedback that you need?
4. Do the same for your relationship. What did you have in common? What is different?

Act

1. What areas do you want to change for yourself?

2. How can you work to minimize any impact that the culture has had on you?
3. How can you adjust for future impact or spillover?
4. What support do you need from your spouse to make these changes?
5. How can you support your spouse in their changes?
6. What adjustments are you as a couple willing to make for your relationship to minimize the impact and spillover and move forward to make the relationship you both desire?
7. What support do you need for your relationship goals?

CONNECTED

There are real challenges to connection in relationships that are impacted by law enforcement culture. There are the obvious challenges of time and the ability to talk for a length of time whether it is due to shifts, sleeping, the downside of the hypervigilance cycle, or emotional numbing. Conditioning also impacts connection due to the mindset of fixing, reacting to a situation, the struggle of emotional vulnerability, the inability to access emotions, which can impact the ability to connect in empathy.

Expect more in regard to connection in your relationship. We are each other's greatest support and we need to support each other in a deep and connected way. Sexual intimacy and connection can be challenging due to schedules. You can fit sex into your relationship. There is something deeper and connecting when you have emotionally connected sex. Staying emotionally connected with each other can increase the amount of sexual availability of partners. I tell people, you have to keep the relationship on "simmer" and a "low boil". When you do that, it makes it easy to turn up the heat! By the way, do not plan to have sex. Instead, plan to make time to connect and open up the opportunity to connect sexually.

ACTION STEPS:

Assess

1. In what way do you hold back from your spouse?
2. What do you wish your spouse knew about you or your life that you think they do not know or understand?
3. In thinking over the last week, what does your partner need to know about your world and emotional state that you have not shared.
4. List 3 ways you do not want to be perceived by your spouse.
5. What do you think about the conversation that you currently have with your spouse?
6. What are the dreams that you have for the future? What dreams do you have that you have not been able to fulfil from the past?
7. What are your anxieties about being in a relationship in law enforcement?
8. What do you need from your spouse to be more emotional, open and trust your spouse?

Discuss

1. Share your responses and have your spouse share their responses.
2. Listen closely to each other's responses.
3. Validate something for your spouse. What do you "get" or understand more deeply about your spouse's world?
4. What are emotions you hear your spouse sharing? What emotions do you have in common?

Act

1. Set up times to have more meaningful conversation with each other.
2. Set up times to play together and have fun.
3. Develop your relationship compass if you have not. If you have, how will you stay focused on it?
4. Think of ways to understand your partner in a deeper way and get curious.

Improve Your Emotional Vocabulary: A research [1]study conducted between Paul Eckman, consultant for the movie Inside Out, and Berkley University found that most Americans could only list an average of 3 emotions. In order to be more emotionally connected to your spouse and your own feelings, improve your emotional vocabulary. I have included a list in the back of the book to help you grow your vocabulary and use when you are in conversation with your spouse.

Improve Your Empathy: In order to improve your ability to empathize, you have to have an awareness of some of your own feelings. Pick one or 2 feelings to practice with at a time. Think of a time in your life that you have felt that feeling, notice how it feels, and remember it. When you listen to your spouse, guess what they might be feeling based upon their story, facial expression, and tone. Simply say, "that must have felt ______________". Done! You have worked on connecting through empathy.

Videos to watch: There are 3 videos that I encourage you to watch to help with empathy and emotional vulnerability: Brené Brown's TedX Talk on Vulnerability, RSA Brené Brown Empathy video, and It's Not About the Nail. I also have these videos linked on my website.

COMPASSIONATE

Compassion is impacted in the officer by the continual exposure to the negative side of humanity and trauma. Spouses are also impacted by these elements. Officers are also more likely to be prone to want to fix the problem and become frustrated if they cannot. Research also shows that officers do not like to experience uncomfortable emotions. Many times, officers will dismiss a spouse's feelings or emotions especially if they are negative. As spouses, sometimes it is really uncomfortable when the officer we know is struggling.

Compassion involves implementing many elements of the Sound Relationship House including fondness and admiration, positive perspective, turning toward your partner, validating your partner's perspective, and empathy. It involves emotional vulnerability at times, getting curious, and providing a generous explanation to situations rather than jumping to conclusions. Compassion also includes understanding your partner's world and standing in their shoes without judgement.

Assess

1. What are ways that you judge others? Yourself?
2. What are ways that you judge your spouse? How does this impact your respect, admiration or fondness of your spouse?
3. What information do you need about your partner's story or behavior to reduce the judgement?
4. What emotions or subjects are most uncomfortable for you to listen to in your relationship?
5. What do you see as emotional strength? What do you see as emotional weakness?
6. What part of your partner's world or shoes do you not get?

Discuss

1. Share your answer with your spouse where you feel comfortable doing so.
2. Listen to your spouse's responses and ask questions where you need to understand their biases or judgements.
3. Try to answer your spouse's questions regarding your world.
4. Try to be open and honest about where your judgements come from. Dig deep. Is there a reason for the judgement from an earlier time in your past?

Act

1. What are ways that you both would like to have compassion in the future.
2. How would you like to express and share compassion as a couple?
3. How does compassion relate to your relationship compass?

COURAGEOUS

Officers must confront situations at work. They walk into danger while others are running out of it. Spouses trust and show courage when their officer is at work, trusting they will come home. It takes courage to live separate lives, trusting you will continually come back together. Courage within the couple is impacted at times by the spillover from law enforcement. The conditioning to react to situations can cause eggshells within a relationship and emotional distance as well as the physical distance to grow. Officers and spouses are confronted with the possibility of mental health struggles related to traumatic incidents. We may look strong and brave, but numbing and foreboding joy can get in the way of the true courage it takes to have a connected and intimate relationship.

Courage involves vulnerability. As a couple, we must also be willing to walk into the conflict. We must also be willing to have difficult conflictual conversation. Confrontation is how couples can grow in connection, trust, and intimacy. When a topic or situation is confronted it may be painful initially but heal in a positive way. Without the opportunity for the conflict, wounds can fester and impact the relationship negatively. While this is true for all couples, law enforcement couples must many times overcome the conditioned response in an officer to react rather than listen. Have the courage to lean into emotion and difficult conversation. Have the courage to say "no" to what does not work for your relationship and the courage to say "yes" to that which feels supportive and nurturing to the relationship.

Assess

1. What difficult conversations have you avoided?
2. What is your fear in bringing up the avoided conversations? In other words, what causes you to need courage to speak up?
3. In what ways do you think you exhibit courage in your relationship?
4. In what ways do you think your partner exhibits courage in your relationship?
5. What would you like to have the courage to say "no" to more to support or enhance your relationship?
6. What would you like to have the courage to incorporate or say "yes" to that would enhance or support your relationship.
7. What would you really like your partner to say "no" and "yes" to?
8. What numbing, foreboding joy, or perfection tendencies do you see in yourself and your partner? How would life be different without those tendencies for you? Your partner?

Discuss

1. As a couple, share your answers.
2. As you listen to your partner, listen for content and feelings. Share what you heard about the content and the feelings your partner expressed. "I heard you say ________ and that it felt ________."
3. Express appreciation to your partner for sharing their responses. "I really appreciate you (telling, sharing, expressing, opening up) __________. I know it probably felt __________. (Or It makes me feel __________ (trusted, close to you, cared for) that you shared with me.)

Act

1. As a couple, agree upon 1 or 2 things you want to say "no" to in order to improve the relationship.
2. Repeat #1 with "yes".
3. Plan to bring up and discuss one of the difficult conversations that your partner needs to have.
4. Review Dr. Gottman's [2]Four Horsemen. Be aware of what Horseman you use and use the antidote instead. Go to holdthelinebook.com for more information about the Four Horsemen.
5. Share something emotionally difficult with your spouse during the week.
6. Communicate an appreciation of your spouse at least twice during the week.

COUNTER THE IMPACT

It can be difficult to stay on track with all the elements of law enforcement life as well as life in general. Don't be a victim to it! Officers have defensive tactics they practice and utilize. Couples need to do the same, otherwise known as resilience. Code4Couples® are resilient and continually assess where they are personally, with their spouse, and their relationship compass!

APPLY THE OODA LOOP TO YOUR RELATIONSHIP!

Observe: Gather information about you including mental and emotional state. Observe information about your spouse and the status of the relationship. Stand in your partner's shoes.

Orient: Make sense of the missing information. Get curious about anything you don't understand. Are there stories you are telling yourself? What do you remember about the needs of your partner? Apply a generous explanation if necessary. What do you know from the previous situation? Think about potential options, previous interactions, and your relationship compass.

Decide: Decide what to do. Based upon what you thought about in the Orient stage, decide what to do. No decision is perfect, so do the best you can for your spouse and the relationship. If nothing, go back to Observe.

Act: Act upon your decision. Go back to Observe.

The OODA loop can be applied in all types of situations in your relationship:

- Coming home after shift.
- When you are off duty and need to integrate into the family.
- When you haven't heard from your spouse in a while.
- When it seems that activity or communication is different between you.
- When deciding if an action is right for your relationship.
- When keeping your relationship on course and not being a victim to the impact of law enforcement!

These five elements are vital to the success of your relationship and your well-being. There are many individual unique elements to each of these categories, but continually assessing them will help you, as a couple, to better understand and control the individual's aspects of the relationship that may be suffering and need attention. It is helpful to know where you are excelling and the part that needs a little extra attention and improvement. Utilize the assessments for your relationship on a regular basis and choose new or proven action steps to get or stay Code 4!

WE STILL AREN'T PERFECT

We are watching a show on TV. He's on his phone and it looks like he's scrolling. My immediate thought is he is bored and entertaining himself on his new Instagram account and looking at wine and food. (One of our hobbies) I'm annoyed and make a snarky comment about him watching the show with me instead of being on his phone. He turns to me and tells me how someone in the show mentioned something about something and he wanted to research it some more. He then goes on to tell me what he has learned. *Fail*! My story got the best of me.

He, on the other hand, was in it for the *win*! He totally extended the benefits of the doubt to me. He knew what was going on with me and chose not to react but instead walk into my world and let me know that he *was* with me. He was connecting but needed to also satisfy a curiosity.

I'm not always good about stating my feelings and what I need or what I am thinking. It is still a relatively new skill for me and I'm working on it.

My husband continues to work on reacting. I work on being on his team and not trying to shut down his feelings. There are times when he will say something and I will raise my left eye brow fairly high. Just the one. He will look at me and say, "Let me try that again." It's become a little joke between us. We continue to work on owning up to our own behavior. When we do, we truly apologize and not in some off-handed way. I am most appreciative of him taking the time to understand what it is like in my world. Standing in each other's shoes will add an incredible amount into your "love" bank account. Even if it isn't exactly right, the attempt of understanding goes a long way between the two of us as I know it will for you.

I find it overwhelming at times to sit and think about the challenges we face in our law enforcement relationships. Every day the law enforcement spouse extends trust to the world that their officer is going to come home. Every day the officer walks out the door trusting that their family will be safe while they are out protecting the rest of the community, knowing that if something goes wrong they will not be able to be there. Every day the officer goes to work and makes a commitment to come back home but deep insides shoves away the nagging feeling of "maybe not." That scenario in itself would have many people backing out of the relationship.

YOU CHOOSE TO STAY

You have all of the aspects of marriage that are challenging for everyone such as connection, trust, commitment, and conflict. Let's add on to that the impact of trauma whether a critical incident, operational stress injury, or delayed onset of chronic exposure, psychological conditioning, mindset shifts, hypervigilance, and the impact on the limbic system and amygdala. Let's also add on the societal pressure and scrutiny into the mix. I look at it written down and realize that it is no wonder that relationships struggle and that I hit a wall as I'm sure you do at times.

When we walked down the aisle together, we had ideas that our relationship would have ups and downs due to a career in law enforcement. We had some idea that the schedule would suck and we would miss out on holidays. We knew there was a potential for physical injury. We knew there would probably be some stress and strain. We had absolutely no idea both of us would be impacted psychologically. We had no idea how the job would spillover over into our relationship in such a covert way. It was there under the surface and infiltrating without our permission or knowledge.

Some aspects like shift work, sleep schedules, and critical incidents made sense to us. When you don't see each other for days or sometimes weeks at a time, it is hard to reconnect in a meaningful way. It's like starting over or trying to play catch up over a long period of time and it's difficult to recall what has happened during that period of time. Sticky notes and text messages work great but connecting conversation must be intimate and meaningful. What was meaningful conversation one day was being discussed with other people that were there in the moment with availability.

It's easy to get caught in the trap of who has it worse or who is making the bigger sacrifice rather than understanding that while the sacrifice is different, they are equally necessary and admired. It can be easy to let contempt and resentment get in the way and compare how other couples get to spend time together, don't have as many hurdles, or are just more "normal." It can even flow into being critical of each other or shutting each other out of the feelings.

Guilt and shame can sneak in and causes us to protect ourselves or not share. Guilt over getting to enjoy time away from each other. Guilt for not being together or sharing moments of importance. Shame for not supporting each other. Shame for having negative feelings about our spouse or positive ones toward someone else. Breaking all this down can cause anyone to feel overwhelmed by the magnitude of elements necessary to maintain a relationship much less overcome the psychological elements created by years in law enforcement.

But not you!

You are now armed with the knowledge you need to understand and protect your relationship.

You have tools to assess and make changes in connection and communication. You have action steps you can implement to make changes as needed.

You don't need to remember everything all the time. There are a few messages that can help to remind you of the main points for you to keep in mind and positively impact your relationship.

You know that whether it is the time apart or a critical incident, there is going to be some impact to you as an officer or spouse. You understand that conditioning and continual exposure to negative experiences are going to have impact. Officers and spouses must be willing to self-assess and be introspective about the impact. Don't allow your brain to "numb" and take charge. Remember: Your brain is there to protect you, not make you happy. You have control of letting it impact you or you decide that it is not going to be *who* you are and just *what* you do.

What keeps an officer safe on the job can impact negatively on life outside of the job.

You know it is up to you not to become a victim of the experiences and instead be the victor! Mindfulness, purpose, and intent are counterweight to the impact. You set up times to debrief and set up rituals to connect with deeper conversation. You are each other's support system. Admitting you are impacted by the career or that you need support and help does not imply weakness. It implies strength and courage.

The body adjusts to protect officers while on the job. What is witnessed and experienced on the job by the body is absorbed by the body. The body learns to numb but this commonly results in the inability to express emotions and connect with others through empathy. It also comes with physical consequences such as struggles sleeping, high blood pressure, and cholesterol. The reactions and beliefs that keep officers safe on the job distance them from those they love most. Hypervigilance can result in conflict, eggshells, sparkly objects, disengagement, and negative behaviors.

You know that officers are conditioned to react, not to respond. This ability to react rather than respond does not turn off once the first responder returns home. Instead, the brain interprets many things first as a threat rather than taking a moment to assess and analyze the situation. You understand that this can cause an officer to react in a larger way than needed or react in a negative way in a situation only to realize, after the fight or flight response has leveled out, that the reaction was out of place. You work to own your individual behavior and give a generous explanation when your partner is struggling.

The time apart can make it easy to get caught up in our own world. You know that just makes connection worse in the relationship. You know that you must work to stand in the shoes of your partner and understand what their world looks like through their eyes. Without an understanding of what is potentially happening emotionally, couples become more distant, personalize partner's behavior, "eggshells" increase within the relationship, resentment and contempt increases and needs are not met which in turn may lead to affairs, family violence, and divorce. It is not enough to just know the daily occurrences of each other's lives but couples much understand the psychological and biological impact the career has on each other and themselves. What may be happening on the surface could be rooted in something else deeper.

When couples understand what is going on with their partner, they decrease personalization and negative narratives and increase connection and support. This understanding involves "seeing" and "knowing" the person, understanding how they think, are conditioned, the impact of their personal experiences, and knowing their character and heart in order to depersonalize, offer a generous explanation, "turn toward", support, and confront with love.

If we don't stand in each other's shoes, chances are there will not be any shoes left to stand in but your own.

BETTER HOME LIFE EQUALS BETTER WORK LIFE.

In a 2019 research [1]article, 40% of officers surveyed had low levels of Compassion Satisfaction, which means that those officers did not feel satisfied with the help they are providing others, appreciation from those they serve, or valued by those they serve. It is statistics like this that make a positive home life crucial and critical for an officer's mental health. In the case of a first responder, this emotional distraction can lead to safety-related issues, increased risk-taking behavior, and potential injury. When home is not a safe place for first responders, their bodies can remain in a hypervigilant state resulting in a psychological and physical breakdown.

The demands of the job often results in officers being stressed and on the edge of burn out which interferes with the connection to family and spouses. Spouses are also subjected to burn out due to the time alone, stressors from friends and family, and running the household alone much of the time. Stressors at home can, for anyone, have the potential to cause mental distraction. You make sure that home remains a safe place for *both* of you. By standing in each other's shoes, you know what is going on with each other and support each other to make a positive, safe, and resilient place.

IT'S A CALLING BUT IT IS NOT WHO YOU ARE.

Law enforcement lifestyle has the potential to become insular. There is a great sense of pride within our law enforcement community. We associate with those that understand us, whether other officers or spouses. It is comforting to connect with those that understand our experiences, the struggles in our relationships, as well as the criticism that we may be feeling from the outside. It is important to have people around us that can empathize and support us. It is also important to remember that law enforcement is a job, not an identity. It is only a part of who we are as people and as a couple.

You know, just like anything in life, balance and moderation is important. Exposing yourself to other communities, interests, information, and hobbies is essential to the success of thriving while working law enforcement and after retirement.

It's not always the same

Not every officer or partner will be impacted the same way.

Not every behavior is associated with the impact of law enforcement.

Sometimes it is just personality differences, flaws, and aspects of our journey in life that causes us to behave or believe the way we do.

As Freud said, "Sometimes a snake is just a snake."

It is helpful and necessary to understand the impact of law enforcement on your relationship. It does not excuse bad behavior. You are responsible for your own actions and need to own and apologize for what does not honor your spouse or the relationship. You are also responsible for communicating your personal boundaries about behaviors that you believe are disrespectful or hurtful. Furthermore, you are responsible for taking action if the requests are not honored. This can range from something simple like saying, "I'm going to go on a 20 minute walk so we can both calm down before continuing this conversation." to leaving a relationship with a partner that is continually disrespectful to you or the relationship. Knowing what is underneath is helpful to not only understand how to correct the situation but also knowing when your partner is choosing not to do their part.

I have shared information that will help you not only protect your relationship, but guide you through some of the most challenging places in your career in law enforcement, as a couple. You have a reinforced arsenal of tools and weapons to assess and protect your relationship. Resources for the book will continue to be updated at www.holdthelinebook.com You can also check out my podcast and courses at www.code4couples.com

There will continue to be challenges but you can get through it *together*.

You are each other's greatest source of resilience.

The two of you can stand your ground.

You can determine how you need to flex and where you need to stand firm.

You determine where the line is and how much impact is too much impact.

You've got this.

Hold the Line.

ADDENDUM
SURVIVING CRITICAL INCIDENTS

As a law enforcement couple, there will probably be a time that you will experience some type of critical incident, accident, assault (verbal or physical), or near miss. Many times, officers need to stay in the mindset of "not me" in order to go to a job where there is a potential that their life will be threatened.

As spouses, we may rationalize and say, "that happens in other cities" or be told to trust the training. We do this to be able to let our spouses walk out the door and not obsess about all the possible dangers they might face that day.

Then there is the day when that fragile reality is shattered. A call is made.

"Ms. Doyle? I don't want you to panic...."

Or, "Honey, if you watch the news, I'm ok."

Little phrases that make time stop.

Everything slows down.

You experience fear, confusion, bewilderment, panic, and can become completely paralyzed.

You get through the incident. Maybe there are injuries. Maybe there is not. Regardless, there is something different in you.

You feel more fear now.

You dream about the incident, have flashbacks to what you saw or experienced, have gaps in memory, or just can't get your head "back in the game."

If any of this sounds familiar, you have probably experienced a traumatic event.

WHAT IS A TRAUMATIC EVENT OR CRITICAL INCIDENT?

A traumatic event is an event or incident that has some type of harm including emotional, psychological, or physical harm. The event also has to cause the individual to feel threatened, anxious, or frightened and many times, an individual may not know how to respond. As a spouse, your officer can go through an incident and that incident may not be traumatic. You, however, can experience trauma because of their event. Officers, keep in mind that many times your reaction to fear, anxiety, and a threat is displayed as anger when deciding if an event was traumatic.

In speaking to officers who have been through a critical incident, feelings of shame during the incident are often an indicator that the event was traumatic. "I had to ask for help. It was humiliating. I should have been able to do it myself." "Other guys were there with me and they seemed fine. I'm weak for not being able to handle this." "I just keep thinking that if that book wasn't there to have stopped the bullet, I wouldn't be here. I should have covered myself better." All statements I have heard from officers in my office.

We all handle events differently. What impacts one person will not necessarily impact another. We all have different experiences, upbringing, values, beliefs, and pain which impacts the way our brain interprets and processes the information. Those same aspects can impact our resiliency and ability to recover. Someone that struggles with anxiety and then goes through an event may struggle to let the anxious feelings or thoughts go. Someone that experienced danger or trauma as a child may struggle with feeling safe after an event or incident. Someone who has never had to experience any adversity or traumatic event will take more time to process through than someone who has. There is no correct way to handle an event or process through an incident.

WHAT YOU CAN EXPECT TO EXPERIENCE IN YOUR BODY?

People are surprised at the impact that an incident can have on your body and mind. One of my police wife friends contacted me after her husband was in an incident. She called to update me about what happened and then I told her everything that she was probably going to go through and experience. I checked in with her several times over the next week. She told me later she was so grateful that I shared what to expect as it eased her anxiety when she felt those symptoms.

HERE ARE 5 WAYS THAT YOUR BODY IS GOING TO EXPERIENCE A TRAUMATIC EVENT.

1. Your brain's fight or flight system takes over. Your brain will simply take over in some form or fashion when the incident is occurring, which for a spouse can be the minute they find out about the incident. This could be after the incident is "done" for the officer. In fact, the officer might not even see it as an incident. You could have a spouse in fight or flight and an officer saying, "I don't know what the big deal is. I'm home and I'm safe." The brain goes into Fight, Flight, or Freeze.

The freeze mode can look like confusion or an inability to make a decision. The first time I received a phone call, I hung up and sat there wondering if I should go to the hospital or if my husband would think it ridiculous if I came. I was in total "freeze" mode. During this time, your brain will dump cortisol into your system and be prepared to respond. You might feel "buzzy" physically or emotional. Sometimes we might start to "over function" and start coordinating activities, thinking about how to help in the situation, and taking charge. Other people "under function" and can't pull themselves together to do whatever needs to be done.

THIS IS ALL NORMAL.

2. **Your brain needs to recover.** After the initial dumps of cortisol in the fight or flight response, the brain will need to recover. This may be hours later. This may be days later. In recovery, the brain wants to shut down. Your body needs to recover and it will take some time. You may feel "foggy brained" and not be able to think as clearly. You may forget to do simple tasks or just not be able to focus.

Once again, normal.

3. **Your brain will need to process what has happened.** In the moment of the incident, the brain is responding to the crisis, or what is perceived to be a crisis. It then must recover. Only after equalizing again can the brain start to process the information. Fight or Flight occurs in the limbic region of the brain while processing occurs in other regions of the brain. You may find yourself distracted with "what if" thoughts. "What if ________ would have happened."

You may have disturbing dreams or nightmares. You may have flashbacks to the moment when you experienced the event or first heard about it from your officer. When this occurs, the brain is trying to make sense of the situation. It is normal to have dreams and night terrors. These flashbacks and nightmares may feel very real as your body may be reliving the moment with all the senses it experienced in those moments.

The brain is doing its job. It is ok if all these things occur. This also takes time to move through, sometimes weeks and sometimes months.

4. **Your anxiety will probably go up.** You will become more hyper aware or hypersensitive to negative events and have fear responses. The incident has caused your brain to catalog new threats. Your brain is there to keep you safe, not happy. It constantly scans for danger. When an incident occurs, the brain is going to increase it's scanning of the threat and cause the fight or flight response to trigger inappropriately. As I mentioned above, this leads to dumps of cortisol.

When there is nothing to react to, the brain and body will turn on itself which leads to feelings of anxiety or depression. You might feel paranoid at times and overprotective of your spouse or family. This is all a part of your brain starting to process the event and find its new normal.

5. **Life will be different, but you will recover.** A traumatic event usually leaves a scar. Many times, this scar is unseen. As time goes by, most scars fade. Every now and then, you may look at it and remember the pain or hit it and it hurts. The event will be in your brain and when similar incidents occur or you hear about another police spouse struggling with an event, it may bring up the feeling of your own. It's ok.

IS IT PTSD?

Please keep in mind that not every incident is trauma and not every trauma results in PTSD. Post-Traumatic Stress (PTS) or Post Traumatic Stress Disorder (PTSD) has a very specific criteria to meet. I hear people label themselves with the diagnosis because they don't understand that it is normal to struggle for a while after an incident, sometimes for months. I hope that reviewing the information above you understand a little more about the process.

When there is a critical incident, there is the potential of not only PTSD but Secondary Traumatic Stress (STS) as a spouse or officer, or Acute Stress Disorder. If you are struggling, reach out to a mental health professional. Moving through a traumatic event can be difficult and there is no reason to suffer when there are trained professionals that can help provide some relief. PTSD is something that can be minimized and even healed. While it's important to address symptoms quickly, there is no wrong time to seek help. Therapeutic techniques such as Cognitive Processing, EMDR, and ART are all therapies based on research which help to ease and sometimes heal the symptoms of PTSD.

Your body and brain have their own processes in coping and processing a critical incident or traumatic event. Sometimes knowing what is going on takes some of the panic and stress away.

Critical incidents have the potential to cause not only physical injuries but also emotional and psychological injuries. These psychological injuries are not only felt by officers but also spouses. With law enforcement being more of a target, critical incidents may come to include the psychological injury that can occur from enduring hours of people yelling hateful words at you. Seeing someone you love being verbally battered for hours on end would be deemed abuse if it were a relationship which would leave emotional and psychological scars. Spouses are on high alert due to not only media coverage but live streams from events, watching to see if their officer is safe or in danger, or neighbors speaking against police or writing derogatory messages against police on their cars. This creates a fight or flight reaction in spouses as well.

Resiliency matters. Whether you are recovering from a critical incident that involves physical violence or verbal beatings, what we do during and after can positively impact our brain's recovery. If you know tools to use and implement after a critical event, both you and your spouse will not be as deeply impacted in the long term.

Here are 10 ways to help yourself, spouse, or family members move through a critical incident.

1. **Drink Water.** Yup. Lots and lots of water. Remember that cortisol is being released into your system during the event and then for a while after the event when your brain is trying to synthesize it. Water helps to flush out your system. Without water, your body will store the cortisol which will cause weight gain and will also prevent your body's natural sewer system from operating.
2. **Sleep.** The cortisol and stress are taxing on your body and your body needs to recover. When you sleep, not only will your brain be able to process the incident and information, it cleans your brain. Your brain has a sewer system, the glymphatic system, which cleans out the waste and toxins in your brain while you sleep, toxins that are caused from experiences from the day. Flushing these toxins can also help when healing from a traumatic event. If you find yourself lying in bed awake, get up for a while and read a book, write, or do a chore and then return back to bed. Sleep when you can. There are several natural and homeopathic remedies that can be used to assist with sleep which you may want to consider. Try to stay away from

prescription medication if possible. You can also try apps to help such as Calm or Breethe.

3. **Exercise.** Move your body. Do yoga. Walk. Run. Bike. Row. Swim. Surf. Have a silent disco party with your headphones. When you move your body, you will release some of the body/brain's desire to take action. It will see the movement as you taking action.
4. **Breathe.** One of the few ways we can control the fight or flight response is with our breath. If you slow down your breath, specifically your exhales, your heart will slow, and your brain will be signaled that danger has gone. One method is box breathing which was developed by the Navy Seals. In this method, you breath in for 4 seconds, hold for 4 seconds, breath out for 4 seconds, and then hold for 4 seconds. Another method I teach is to use a cocktail straw or a coffee stirrer. Breath in slowly and deeply. Hold for 4 seconds. Then, breath out through the straw. *That* will slow your breathing down.
5. **Give Permission.** You will probably handle the situation differently from your spouse. That needs to be ok. It also needs to be ok if your spouse handles it differently. Some people need to process verbally and talk about it. Other people process internally and just sit and think. Your emotions about the situation are ok. There is no right or wrong way to feel about the event. Emotions or struggling with the event does not make you weak. It is simply different. Be kind to yourself and give yourself and your spouse permission to feel and maybe grieve in their own way. Own the feelings you have and stop judging them. If you are scared, you are scared and talk about it. When we hide and judge our own feelings, it turns into shame not only because of our self judgement and the fear of judgement but because we are now hiding those feelings.

Shame lurks in the dark. It cannot live in the light. You want to work toward healing and not creating more pain.

6. **Talk to Each Other.** As a couple, it is great if you can talk to each other. Officers, there is no weakness in sharing of emotions or fear. Spouses, you don't have to "be strong" all the time either. When you share with each other, it's important to comfort and NOT fix. Validate the other person's feelings. It can feel so good sometimes when you hear someone else say, "this is hard and it sucks".
7. **Talk to Others.** If you are an officer, it is common to talk to others that were at the incident to help to process the event. Make sure you are also sharing with your spouse. Do not leave them out of the loop about how or with whom you are sharing. Spouses, it's important that you have a trusted person that you can process through with as well. Find someone who is willing to let you vent or cry that can be understanding. Many times the more we verbally process, the more our brain can become desensitized to the event. The first several times you talk about it, all the emotions will come up. As you continue to talk about it, it won't be quite as emotional, and you might even tire of talking about it. *[Note: There are times when I see emotional affairs pop-up with officers or spouses when they start leaning on someone that could potentially be a romantic partner. Make sure you have your boundaries clear and you are being transparent with conversations.]*
8. **Don't Feed the Gremlin.** This is an old reference from the movie Gremlins. In the movie, the cutest little creature, Gizmo, multiplied if he got water on him and turned into a Gremlin if you fed him after dark. Gremlins were nasty creatures that wreaked havoc on everything. The same goes for your brain. Remember, your brain is there to keep you safe, not make you happy. We are *wired* for fear. We don't need to feed it more fear-based thoughts. Be aware of how

much time you are thinking about the "what ifs" and shut them down as quickly as possible. Stay focused on the here and now. Focus on what you can do in that moment instead of focusing on the past or the future.

9. **Tell Your Brain to Stand Down**. Think of your brain and your mind as two different things. If your brain is keeping you safe, it may be trying to warn you about something. This is actually where our anxiety comes from. The fact is that sometimes our brain tries to alert us to situations that just aren't necessary. Let's take spilt milk. Our brain hears the glass land on the table and causes you to jump sometimes out of your seat. Sometimes our brains react verbally and say things like, "Pay attention. Oh *my gosh*!" Eventually, we realize... it's just milk. Our brains are going to react to the milk many times the same way as if there was a real threat. You can tell your brain to stand down. The best phrase that I learned was from Olivia from Yoga for First Responders. In the class, she had us hold a pose until we were straining and then say, "This is a challenge *not a threat*". She explained by putting us in the challenging poses and then saying the phrase, we were teaching our brain to stand down. That the situation was challenging, but not threatening. Try it out for yourself when you start to feel anxious, overwhelmed, or your thoughts start to wander.
10. **Gratitude.** The practice of gratitude can help to combat the brain's natural negative way of thinking. Anytime you find yourself slipping into the negative or feeling anxiety, think of things for which you are grateful. You can find gratitude just about anywhere. Find something you are grateful for. At the moment of writing this, I'm grateful for my ceiling fan, a glass of sweet tea, a fly swatter, and my dog snoring away. Just writing that brings me a little lift and a moment of "ahhh" in my life. Gratitude helps you find

those cracks of sunshine and thus, hope in dark moments. It is a necessary part of the resilience you need to heal from the event.

If you apply these 10 principles, you will have a great start to your recovery from a critical incident as an officer or the spouse of an officer.

REFERENCES

WHAT WE ALL KNOW…. BUT WHY?

1. Mccoy, Shawn P., and Michael G. Aamodt. "A Comparison of Law Enforcement Divorce Rates with Those of Other Occupations." *Journal of Police and Criminal Psychology* 25, no. 1 (October 20, 2009): 1–16. https://doi.org/10.1007/s11896-009-9057-8.
2. Garcia-Rada, Ximena, Ovul Sezer, and Michael I. Norton. "Rituals and Nuptials: The Emotional and Relational Consequences of Relationship Rituals." *Journal of the Association for Consumer Research* 4, no. 2 (March 6, 2019): 185–97. https://doi.org/10.1086/702761.
3. Porter, Krystin L., and Richard C. Henriksen. "The Phenomenological Experience of First Responder Spouses." *The Family Journal* 24, no. 1 (2015): 44–51. https://doi.org/10.1177/1066480715615651.

THE UNDERPINNING

1. Gilmartin, Kevin M. Emotional Survival for Law Enforcement: a Guide for Officers and Their Families. Tucson, AZ: E-S Press, 2002, pg 35.
2. Sharps, Matthew Joseph. "This Is Your Brain on Adrenaline: The Nervous System, Long-Term Stress, and The World of Law Enforcement." Essay. In *Processing under Pressure: Stress, Memory and Decision-Making in Law Enforcement*, 5–24. Flushing,, NY: Looseleaf Law Publications, Inc., 2017.
3. Gilmartin, Kevin M. Emotional Survival for Law Enforcement: a Guide for Officers and Their Families. Tucson, AZ: E-S Press, 2002, Pg 43.
4. Gilmartin, Kevin M. *Emotional Survival for Law Enforcement: a Guide for Officers and Their Families*. Tucson, AZ: E-S Press, 2002.
5. Gilmartin, Kevin M. Emotional Survival for Law Enforcement: a Guide for Officers and Their Families. Tucson, AZ: E-S Press, 2002, Pg 26-31

SPILLOVER

1. Tuttle, Brooke Mcquerrey, et al. "Stress Spillover in Policing and Negative Relationship Functioning for Law Enforcement Marriages." *The Family Journal*, vol. 26, no. 2, Apr. 2018, pp. 246–252., doi:10.1177/1066480718775739.
2. Gottman, John Mordechai. "Chronic DPA and Immunosuppression." Essay. In *The Marriage Clinic: a Scientifically-Based Marital Therapy*, 104–6. New York: W.W. Norton & Company, 1999.

3. Garcia-Rada, Ximena, Ovul Sezer, and Michael I. Norton. "Rituals and Nuptials: The Emotional and Relational Consequences of Relationship Rituals." *Journal of the Association for Consumer Research* 4, no. 2 (March 6, 2019): 185–97. https://doi.org/10.1086/702761.

THE CONFLICT

1. Gottman, John, and Nan Silver. *The Seven Principles for Making Marriage Work: a Practical Guide from the Country's Foremost Relationship Expert*. Toronto, ON: Random House, 1999, 7.
2. Gottman, John Mordechai. *Principia Amoris: the New Science of Love*. New York, NY: Routledge, 2015.
3. Gottman, John Mordechai. *Principia Amoris: the New Science of Love*. New York, NY: Routledge, 2015.
4. Gottman, John Mordechai., and Julie Schwartz. Gottman. *Level 1 Clinical Training Gottman Method Couples Therapy: Bridging the Couple Chasm*. Seattle, WA: Gottman Institute, 2017.

INTIMACY – WHAT DOESN'T WORK

1. Brown, Brené. "The Power of Vulnerability." TED, June 2010. https://www.ted.com/talks/brene_brown_the_power_of_vulnerability?language=en.
2. Brown, C. Brené. *I Thought It Was Just Me (but It Isn't): Making the Journey from "What Will People Think?" to "I Am Enough"*. New York, NY: Gotham, 2007.
3. Brown, C. Brené. *I Thought It Was Just Me (but It Isn't): Making the Journey from "What Will People Think?" to "I Am Enough"*. New York, NY: Gotham, 2007.
4. Brown Brené. *Daring Greatly: How the Courage to Be Vulnerable Transforms the Way We Live, Love, Parent, and Lead*. New York, NY: Avery, 2015.
5. Wiseman, Theresa. "An Concept Analysis of Empathy." *Journal of Advanced Nursing* 23, no. 6 (1996): 1162–67. https://doi.org/ 10.1046/j.1365-2648.1996.12213.x.

SO NOW WHAT?

1. Garcia-Rada, Ximena, Ovul Sezer, and Michael I. Norton. "Rituals and Nuptials: The Emotional and Relational Consequences of Relationship Rituals." *Journal of the Association for Consumer Research* 4, no. 2 (March 6, 2019): 185–97. https://doi.org/10.1086/702761.

HEROES DON'T DO IT ALONE®

1. Conn, Stephanie M. 2018. Increasing Resilience in Police and Emergency Personnel Strengthening Your Mental Armor. Milton: Routledge, pg 5.
2. Conn, Stephanie M. 2018. Increasing Resilience in Police and Emergency Personnel Strengthening Your Mental Armor. Milton: Routledge, pg 5.
3. Papazoglou, K., Koskelainen, M., & Stuewe, N. (2019). Examining the Relationship Between Personality Traits, Compassion Satisfaction, and Compassion Fatigue Among Police Officers. SAGE Open, 9 (1)
4. Conn, Stephanie M. 2018. Increasing Resilience in Police and Emergency Personnel Strengthening Your Mental Armor. Milton: Routledge, pg 141.

MAKING YOUR RELATIONSHIP CODE 4

1. Keltner, Dacher, and Paul Ekman. "The Science of 'Inside Out'." The New York Times. The New York Times, July 3, 2015. https://www.nytimes.com/2015/07/05/opinion/sunday/the-science-of-inside-out.html?partner=socialflow.
2. Gottman, John, and Nan Silver. *The Seven Principles for Making Marriage Work: a Practical Guide from the Country's Foremost Relationship Expert*. Toronto, ON: Random House, 1999, 32.

WE STILL AREN'T PERFECT

1. (Papazoglou, K., Koskelainen, M., & Stuewe, N. (2019). Examining the Relationship Between Personality Traits, Compassion Satisfaction, and Compassion Fatigue Among Police Officers. SAGE Open, 9(1))

ABOUT THE AUTHOR

Cyndi Doyle is a Licensed Professional Counselor Supervisor and National Board Certified Counselor, certified in Critical Incident Stress Management (CISM), and serves teams in the DFW area. She is also a law enforcement spouse of over 20 years.

She was inspired to create Code4Couples® when, as a mental health professional and couple's counselor, she struggled to understand what was happening in her relationship and her husband. She now works to normalize, educate, and empower law enforcement couples to have connected and resilient relationships.

Cyndi is known for engaging presentations through combining her personal story, sense of humor, knowledge, and experience. She educates audiences on her Code4Couples® podcast and at presentations to local and national police association conferences.

In 2018, the State of Texas Governor's Office selected Cyndi as one of three mental health professionals to serve on a statewide work group focusing on Mental Health Access for First Responders.

Her most recent awards include the Samuel T. Gladding Unsung Heroes Award by the American Counseling Association, recognizing her contribution to first responder mental health and the mental health field.

To learn more or connect with Cyndi, visit www.Code4Couples.com or www.HoldtheLineBook.com.

CPSIA information can be obtained
at www.ICGtesting.com
Printed in the USA
BVHW040552300321
603700BV00016BA/717